FROM
APPRENTICE
TO
CEO

A Complete Guide to the Hospitality Industry

FROM APPRENTICE TO CEO

A Complete Guide to the Hospitality Industry

LOUIS SAILER

Notion Press

Old No. 38, New No. 6,

McNichols Road, Chetpet,

Chennai - 600 031

First Published by Notion Press 2015

Copyright © Louis Sailer 2015

All Rights Reserved.

ISBN: 978-93-5206-407-6

This book is dedicated to Kelly and Madison, my beautiful wife and gorgeous daughter who made it possible for me to make this career and still, be able to dedicate, my passion to the endless hours required for my guests, patrons and staff all year around.

CONTENTS

THAT GUEST OF YOURS

THE HUMAN NATURE

IN OPERATIONS

INTRODUCTION

All aspiring luxury hotel professionals can use an extra career tip once in a while. This book (Volume I) is a compilation of hands-on experiences and real-life scenarios that I have accumulated from my work as a professional in the luxury hospitality industry in Europe, the United States, Japan, Singapore, China, and the Caribbean. Volume II to follow since London and India.

This book focuses on the most important issues that everyone, from Apprentice to General Managers, face today. All the examples and scenarios provide helpful real-time suggestions and recommendations regarding the important factors that can lead to a successful career in the industries for luxury hospitality, tourism and gastronomy.

Who Should Read this Book?

This book offers not only career advice and is a grab bag of topics, thoughts and help for all hotel, resort, restaurant, catering, gastronomy and service professionals, regardless of age and rank, but also aims at general readers that like to see this business from the other side and are curious about how this business works. It provides an arsenal of tips, guidance, examples, and short stories of what should, can, and should not be done throughout a person's career in the hospitality industry.

The know-how shared in this book arise from 2½ decades of experience in the luxury hotel and restaurant industry in such notable places and countries as California, Hawaii, the Caribbean, Singapore, Germany, Austria, Japan, and China. This book is an invaluable tool that provides upfront advice and hard-won insights that can be used for a lifetime.

Taking a short break halfway through my career, I decided to partially chronicle my professional experiences and share my knowledge with others, who I hope can benefit from it for generations to come.

The book is categorized by chapters that discuss a topic, provide a down to earth career tip, and build up as the examples progress. The beginning chapters represent the early stages in one's career while the progressive and latter parts are useful for managers of today or aspiring professionals in the making.

Either way, the book can be read from front to back or back to front. Intended as a life-long keeper, I sincerely hope that many people can benefit from it and help the luxury hotel industry to return to its famed and trustworthy origins.

CAREER BASICS

1 Knowledge Fundamentals

Over the course of one's career, there are many levels of knowledge that one needs to obtain in order to advance professionally. I would like to discuss three of these basics: basic knowledge, fundamental knowledge, and professional knowledge. Success begins with your ability to ask a question. If you get an answer, you have gained a bit more information and are, thus, about to be able to master the basic knowledge level. Now, with that knowledge in hand, you will be able to ask additional questions that are more in-depth. Doing so will deepen your understanding of a specific topic and further enhance your basic knowledge level skills. It will also prepare you to advance to the fundamental knowledge level. The fundamental knowledge level provides you with a solid foundation for knowing more about a specific topic. Here is a tip for succeeding at this level: it is important to aspire more, dig deeper, and try to find out everything there is to know about that topic. If you keep striving for more information, you will eventually reach a professional or expert knowledge level. Once that level of subject mastery is reached and everything is known about the ins and outs of a particular subject, one will feel good and full of the confidence.

Career Tip: Building a progressive urge for knowledge at an early stage is very important. The brain is an endless space that can hold a lot of information. The more you fill it up, in the early years of your career, the more successful you will be down the road as your career advances. Never stop.

---

2 Simply Cheese

Well, it may not be that simple after all. Here is the story: Imagine yourself working in one of, if not the best, restaurant in Europe at the time. You are ten days into your new job, it is during the lunch shift, and, as luck would have it, you get the most regular lunch customer of the restaurant. This is what happened to me. Everything was smooth, from pre-order to appetizer, fish course, and main course. Then came dessert, and the gentleman wanted cheese. Sure! No big deal — with the exception that the cheese board had 45 different cheeses from all-over Europe and a breadbasket with 15 different loafs.

After ten days on the new job, the last thing on my mind had been to study the cheeses so I bluffed and said to one of my more senior colleagues, "Tell me about these five cheeses and that should be sufficient to land the sale."

The commis (young apprentice) set the stage by setting two giant cheese trays in front of the customer and placing the breadbasket behind me. Now it was my turn and I went for the attack, trying to leave the customer little chance to decide, by simply overwhelming him with my five-cheese knowledge. However, after four negative signals with his head and a fifth coming up, I quickly realized that this particular customer knew his cheeses. Now, all of a sudden, I was no longer in attack mode but rather in defensive mode, trying to read the location of the cheese by the direction of his eyes. I had to look at his eyes because I had no idea of the meaning of the French words that he was throwing at me.

To cut a long story short, I never made it to the breadbasket. In the middle of not being able to locate his cheese preference, I gave up, politely and professionally excused myself, and asked a colleague to help me out, which he did with a smile. While I was deeply embarrassed on the one hand, the guest had a ball putting a young chap like me in his place. Lunch service was finished and no one said a word. However, deep down, I knew that everyone was amused and I had this desperate urge not to linger in defeat but to overcome my embarrassment.

Thus, I went to the director of the restaurant, who smiled at me (knowing that I had made a 'booboo') and asked me what my request was. It was simple — to learn as fast as possible about cheese. He lifted his head, thought for a moment, and then asked me how serious I was about my request. I reassured him that I was very serious. He said all right and clarified that it would not be easy and that some of my free time would have to be invested. I agreed and he picked up the phone that very moment.

His conversation started with him saying that he had a young man with him who wished to learn about cheese and who was available at the disposal of the person on the other end of the line. He finished his conversation and looked at me. Then he said, "Your lessons start right now and will take four days."

Kind of taken aback by the quickness with which he had found a solution, I agreed and asked what was next. He gave me an address in the city and told me to report there within 30 minutes. I changed from my uniform into regular clothes and off I went. Upon arrival, I was somewhat surprised to see it was a very small shop. Here again, never underestimate what you do not know. I walked in and introduced myself. An elderly gentleman came up to me and verified my name.

He smiled and quickly changed into a very professional mode, saying, "Not much time, young man. Are you ready?" I was ready — more ready than I had ever been previously. We began with the basics, which, as it turned out, was already way over my basic knowledge level. We dug deeper and deeper, and after four days of returning to his shop and lessons every afternoon, I was personally amazed by how much knowledge you are able to accumulate if you are interested and eager. By the time I ended my sessions, I knew pretty much everything that there was to know about cheese, from cow, goat, and ewe milk, to brushed, washed, with or without ash, with hay, buried in soil for God knows how long, and much more. The week after my lessons, I volunteered — well actually, I forced myself — to work on every cheese board order that the restaurant received. It was suddenly pure satisfaction to be armed with heavy knowledge about a subject or product and to be able to please the customers with confidence.

One day, I challenged a customer to try all 45 cheeses and he agreed. Thereafter, I cut a small piece of each and laid them out in a clockwise direction. I worked my way around the plate, starting at 6 o'clock, each cheese grew in flavor and intensity, ensuring that no cheese would cancel the other out and that a full escalating experience of flavor would be the end result. Of course, I would also match the 15 different loafs of bread for each stage of changing flavors.

Ironically a year later, I had lunch in London at England's best restaurant, and when the cheese board came (unfortunately, it had only 25 cheeses!), I gave the young chap who served me and who seemed unsure about all the cheeses, the same experience that I had endured a year earlier. I hope that he then did the same with his free time as I had done.

3 Values

Everyone has his or her own values. If your personal values are aligned with the values of the company for which you work, you will increase your chances of realizing a successful partnership and a prosperous career. Personal and business relationships are always successful if both sides like each other. Thus, if you frequently upgrade your skills and, consequently, add more value to your company, partnerships between both parties will be in harmony and can make you a more indispensable asset to your company.

Career Tip: Companies value dedicated and devoted staff. If you are happy and deliver a great performance, in addition to your positive attitude, a swift career is in the making. If you are unhappy, if you show no initiative and miss opportunities to upgrade your professional skills and knowledge base, it will negatively affect and hinder your career growth.

4 Integrity

Integrity is one of the most important virtues a company looks for in an employee or a manager. The success of any business lies in the integrity of its staff. When an employee's integrity is called into question, second chances are seldom given. Even the smallest violations can result in immediate reprimand and possible dismissal from employment. Unfortunately, life can bring many unexpected and pitiful examples, such as the really nice and well-liked employee who decided to embezzle that extra cash or the person who feels that a job brings automatic entitlement to the company's products (whether that is a stapler, a calculator, or something of even greater value to the company). The bottom line is that everything in the workplace belongs to the company's owner. Even one ounce of coffee grounds, for that needed morning cup of coffee from the company's espresso machine, is considered pilferage.

Career Tip: While no one is perfect, never think twice that a company will look the other way if you are not conducting business with integrity. There are many temptations in the hospitality industry, but charting a clear, integrity-filled course is the formula for success. If the line is ever crossed, your professional image and reputation could be obliterated forever.

5 Nothing Less Than 100%

Throughout the course of your professional career, always give 100% to any task or project presented to you. Never allow yourself to accept personal mediocrity. Through the course of your workday, if you encounter something that does not seem right and you do not immediately rectify it, you tacitly accept mediocrity. A mediocre work performance means that you are not diligently committed to "walking the talk." Mediocrity adversely affects everyone in the company. When your actions do not match the highest values of integrity and quality, your employees and co-workers will no longer think highly of you. This rule of giving 100% all the time is one of the most essential elements of leadership. Therefore, always live by your own words and lead by example every day.

Career Tip: It is not easy to commit yourself to giving 100% every day, but nothing less than a 100% mindset is required to succeed in the luxury hospitality industry. Giving 100% all the time is an essential part of the luxury hospitality Code of Conduct. It takes training and determination to go the extra mile every day, but once this proactive attitude becomes a habit, it will fuel a successful career.

6 Professional Ingredients

What makes a good professional? The right mindset, also known as a positive attitude, plays a crucial role in a successful career. When this right mindset is combined with a healthy portion of ambition and passion, the doors to many opportunities can be opened. Performing at a high quality level is assured if you perfect your skills and talents and then make it a habit to utilize them every day in the work place. It is popularly believed that if you repeat a task 21 times, it will get embedded in you for life. If you become good, or great, at what you do and always behave in a professional manner, people will recognize and respect you.

Career Tip: You must be fully dedicated to your goals and objectives. The more knowledgeable you are about your industry, your field, or product and the more experience you can draw upon to deliver the necessary solutions to meet your company's challenges and concerns, the greater your credibility will be within your company and among your co-workers and your peers. To be a true professional, you must not only deliver a great performance within your immediate workplace, you must also conduct yourself professionally when dealing with people at all levels of the company and with your company's customer base.

7 Practice

Habits, or permanent quality assurance, come about in many ways, but habits are primarily accomplished through consistent practice. Throughout life, people will continually learn new things. The more a person repeats or practices the new skill, task, or process, the more comfortable he or she will become in executing it. In your career or professional life, repetitive tasks will begin on the first day of work and will only become more complex as your career, and your life, progresses. As a matter of fact, in life, the early tasks are as important as the later tasks. They each set the stage for future behavior.

Career Tip: Repeating tasks will instill confidence and enable you to perform any task to the best of your abilities. The company president, your manager, your co-workers, your subordinates, and your customers always like to see consistency and they appreciate when tasks are completed correctly and on time. Thus, even if you become an executive one day, never forget how important those early tasks are to a job well done. This will enable you to step into any scenario and even, occasionally, to show newcomers how to execute the tasks correctly.

8   Sticking to Your Word

Your reputation is only as good as the promises you keep. Keep the promises you make to your supervisors, employees, co-workers, and customers and follow through with integrity and action. Nobody respects or admires a superficial person who says one thing and does another or who makes a promise but never follows through. Similarly, no one looks up to a person who gives direction or provides leadership and then changes course in midstream. One of the fundamental career goals in the life of a successful professional must be to do what you say you will do.

Career Tip: Think first before you make promises or provide direction and leadership. If you trust that the promise or direction you are about to make or give can be fulfilled, then proceed. If you make promises but fail to keep them, people will no longer think highly of you. If you provide direction or leadership, but change course in the middle of your team's execution, you will create doubt in your capabilities to lead. The bottom line: always stick to your word.

9   Home and Work Rules

Personal conduct in the work place is important. How you present yourself at work and how you interact with others reflect on your professionalism. An old saying cautions: what you do not do at home, do not do in your work place. Do you frequently break your mother's chinaware? Do you disobey your parents' rules when you are in their home? Do you apply a double standard to the way that you interact with friends and loved ones by treating your friends and family differently? If the answer to these questions is "No," but you have caught yourself engaging in these types of behaviors in your workplace, it is time to step back and change the ways in which you interact with others. Failing to do so will negatively affect your career growth opportunities, causing your employer to reprimand you, or even worse, terminate your employment. While first time offenses of making personal use of office supplies or monopolizing a co-workers time with gossiping, may remain unmentioned and forgiven, be aware that, in most cases, they are not forgotten. In the workplace, others notice rude and unprofessional behaviors, even if they do not always comment on it. When you act with integrity and treat others with respect, your personal conduct reflects positively upon you and your company.

Career Tip: In the hospitality industry, the world of luxury requires a certain mindset and impeccable behavior. While the fundamentals of personal conduct are already established at home, it is important to readjust, fine-tune, and apply these behaviors to your new working environment. If you are uncertain about workplace behavioral standards at your place of employment, it is always a good idea to research the available information from the company's human resources department. These guidelines can provide valuable guidance.

10 Academic vs. Apprentice

As professionals, culinary arts and hotel management school graduates and apprentices are on equal footing. While the graduate will begin work with an academic foundation for the fundamental requirements of the job, the apprentice already has hands-on experience in the work environment and, most likely, has mastered a few problem-solving techniques and has fine-tuned their ability to master other tasks. While hotel school graduates need to catch up with regard to real-life work experiences, apprentices need to work on honing their academic skills.

Career Tip: How an employee executes a task and the results that follow will always be the judge of competency and mastery. Culinary arts and hotel management school graduates and on-the-job apprentices each bring to the workplace a distinct set of advantages and disadvantages. Whether you offer experience in craft or academic knowledge in the early stages of your employment, be quick in compensating for the skills and knowledge that you do not possess. Once you are adept in both industry craft and academic knowledge, your professional skills will be more complete and you will be able to more readily progress in your career.

11 Single Craft Specialists

If management is not your forte, becoming a single craft professional is another excellent choice for a hospitality industry career. Throughout the world, there is an extreme shortage of knowledgeable and true hands-on professionals in the luxury hospitality industry. Where have all the professional cooks, waiters, concierges, and housekeepers gone? Nobody knows for sure, but one thing is for certain: it is rare, nowadays, to meet a professional who is well versed and trained in a particular professional field. Highly experienced craftsmen and craftswomen can also demand high salaries in the course of their careers.

Career Tip: Not everyone is cut out for a career in management. Still, there are many other possibilities available to those seeking to reach a high level in the workplace. Every employee is equally important to a company's success, and one department cannot thrive without another. Hence, if you specialize in a particular field or craft, your skills and talents will be as valuable to a company as those of a manager.

12 That Bloody Mary

On an assignment to London, I decided to patronize a bar, not a typical bar, but a very old London-looking one. It was a place with heavy leather furniture, aged brass bolts, a dusty décor, and a bartender, at an age that seemed appropriate with the bar's interior. I am sure that if I would have asked the gentleman for a cosmopolitan, he would have politely obliged; but instead, I asked him for his signature drink.

"A Bloody Mary it is!" he said.

Now it was 7 PM, and a Bloody Mary is not necessarily an evening drink. However, being young and respectful, I said, "Yes, please" (Actually, I had drunk many over my lifetime, but was never was too fond of them).

Then it came. My gums were ready for that sour tomato, lemon, and pepper experience. My first sip ended in dismay. It was unbelievable! The taste, texture, and concoction of the drink were beyond belief. I had never had something so common that tasted so exquisite and beautiful. My mouth was shocked and so was my hotelier's expert ego.

I took the courage to ask the gentleman, easily 30–35 years older than I was, about the drink, and I expressed my absolute enjoyment of it. A bartender, who I had grossly underestimated mere moments ago, had just become my hero.

His bushy, salt and pepper eyebrows rose with joy and he said, "It is in the tomato juice, not the liquor. You can use fine vodka or gin, but the tomatoes are the secret ingredient."

Now, pretty much everyone in the world, with the exception of a very few, was using tomato juice from the can — but he was not. Instead, on top of his normal work schedule, every day before work, he would stop by the local market and hand pick the best tomatoes for his Bloody Mary. Then, he would gently extract the juice and chill just enough to last for his shift.

To date, this gentleman remains close to my heart as an example of true craftsmanship and professional heroism.

13 Career Directions

There are two directions in the industry. One direction is to specialize in a particular profession and become extremely good at it. The other direction is to become a generalist and be able to wear more than one professional hat at a time in order to get the job done. General Managers of luxury hotels used to come predominately from Europe and their employment was predicated upon their professional background in food and beverage or rooms divisions. This has changed over the past two decades. Today, General Managers come from all over the world with professional backgrounds in a variety of fields, such as finance or sales and marketing.

Career Tip: Try to choose your career goal early in life and work hard to achieve it. Be aware that sometimes people make the wrong choice, necessitating a career switch later on in their professional lives. When one has chosen a career that does not suit one's values, goals, or temperament, the decision commonly results in unhappiness, doubt, and a stalled career. However, if you know, deep down, that you have what it takes to succeed in your chosen career path, go for it.

14 Time, Place, and Luck

Time, place, and luck are important elements in any career. However, as with all other things, these elements cannot be controlled. Timing your career steps and choosing the right places take wisdom and a portion of good judgment. On the other hand, luck is a bonus and can help you to be chosen over others who are equally qualified. Theory is easy, and to think that everything will always fall into place as planned is a fragile assumption. Therefore, it is never too early to plan one's path and leave as little as possible up to chance. To excel in your chosen field, constantly set your sights on your objectives and tirelessly work on your goals.

Career Tip: Nothing in life is guaranteed and everyone needs a certain amount of luck to be successful and happy. It is hard to tell how to go about obtaining that luck, but if one never gives up, one increases one's chances of being in the right place at the right time where luck can happen.

15 Road Bumps Ahead

Life is beautiful when you are successful in your career and your world is free from stress and strife. However, there will be moments in your life when unpredictable forces and situations may momentarily derail you. While you may have not seen these challenges coming, in most cases, there are reasons why you have been caught off-guard and unprepared. Bumps in your career path can be a good thing since they will force you to make decisions and to rethink your professional options and strategies.

Career Tip: To master the speed bumps in your career path, you need a strong mindset, determination, and a willingness to learn the lessons offered by the challenges that you face. Given time, patience, and perseverance, all obstacles can be mastered, though some challenges may take a bit longer to overcome than others. When you succeed, it feels good to look back at the speed bump, which is now behind you, and move forward knowing that you learned from your experience and can apply this hard-won, hands-on knowledge to future challenges that may arise.

16 No Pain No Gain

One of the multi-medal winning athletes of the 2010 Winter Olympics was questioned about private life. At the age of twenty-five, the primary memories were not of parties and good times, but of hours, days, months, and years filled with disciplined training, as the old saying goes: "No pain, no gain." This adage applies to all of life's scenarios and every profession in any industry or field. The more determined you are, the higher the probability is that you will succeed. If you are a determined person, the gains that you make will be much greater than the pain you experience along the way.

Career Tip: Self-determination and dedication are some of the toughest components of a hospitality career. This can be especially true when your friends and family are enjoying a holiday weekend and you cannot be with them due to your work commitments. Since the luxury hospitality industry operates 24 hours a day, 365 days each year, working in it will become part of your lifestyle. On a positive side, being off duty when most people are working enables you to go shopping when the malls and shops are not crowded and enjoy a life with few waiting lines. These are just some of the many benefits that come with working in the luxury hospitality industry.

17 Basics That (Must) Get Stuck

Students (or recent graduates), part-time workers, and industry apprentices will always be assigned the most basic tasks when they first begin working in the luxury hospitality field or if they are exploring their career options by working in the industry over their summer holidays. These tasks can range from folding towels to polishing cutlery and from cutting endless buckets of carrots to simply copying documents and much more. While many people begrudgingly fulfill these basic tasks and most fail to see the potential inherent in attending to them, these basic tasks serve an important function. The primary function they fulfill is to familiarize a new employee with their new working environment and to help them feel more comfortable with their new roles and duties. Assigning these basic tasks also provides their employer with the opportunity to assess their work ethic and determine if they are a good fit for the organization. If they do not take these basic tasks seriously, chances are that their employer will not have great faith in their potential with the company.

Career Tip: When one is young, it is difficult to understand why things must be done a certain way. It is important to trust your mentors and teachers; they are equipped with a set of knowledge and skills that you have yet to acquire. If you start a new job, you begin a testing, or probationary, period in which your employer assesses your skills and your work ethic. Learn these basic tasks as quickly and as thoroughly as possible and before you know it, a new chapter in your career will be written.

18 Being Decisive

Entire workplaces and organizations can come to unexpected standstills if decisions are not made promptly or if they are made indecisively. If you are among the employees who must make decisions, make them decisively. If you have doubts, closely examine the situation and apply your best knowledge, good judgment, and common sense as the guiding principles for solving it. Either way, you will soon discover the end result. If your decision will provide benefits to your company's customers or to its task or service oriented areas, chances are you are on the track to success. Never hesitate or be too overcautious since decisions often go awry when handled in this manner.

Career Tip: You must learn how to make decisions early in life. People will depend on you for guidance and directions. Sound decision-making is also a trademark of a good leader. The higher that you rise in your working environment, the more decisions you will eventually have to make. It is human nature to be drawn to decisive decision-makers and leaders.

19 Personalities Change with Uniforms

Most employment positions within the hospitality industry require one to wear a uniform. What is in a uniform? And why does wearing one change people so much? At any bus stop, two individuals could be dressed in shorts, flip-flops, and white T-shirts. At work, they change into their respective uniforms. One dons a janitor's uniform and the other changes into a front office business suit. Suddenly, these people seem to look at one other differently and, so, they act differently with one another. The janitor might become quiet and humble while the businessperson might become arrogant and snobbish. To succeed in any industry, avoid the mistake of judging your co-workers by their uniforms. Both the janitor and the businessperson are equals, and while they may have different job descriptions, their importance to the company lies in the degree to which they successfully perform their tasks, not in their job titles or job descriptions.

Career Tip: No matter how fancy or dull your uniform may be, do not hide or change your proactive, positive personality. Hold your head high and look straight ahead. Greet people of all ranks, even in the back of the house, while passing through work areas. Do not overcompensate by changing your personality based on the type of uniform that you are wearing. Stay natural and be yourself, as doing so will demonstrate your good character and your co-workers and supervisors will respect your integrity and value your leadership.

20 Jump-Start Your Day

If you eagerly wake up every morning and look forward to going to work, then you are probably in the right work environment. Motivation and self-esteem are also easier to come by when you start your day in this way rather than having to drag yourself out of bed in order to get to work every day. Carefully choose your workplace and the departments within your industry since your success relies on your ability to rise and shine and avidly greet each day and the work that lies ahead.

Career Tip: To be successful, be happy and do not let anyone or anything drag you down. Finish what you start each day and, when you walk into your workplace the next morning, you will avoid feeling that unnecessary burden from the incomplete tasks that you did not finish the previous day. Each morning, look in the mirror and smile before beginning your workday. Make sure you wear a permanent.

21 So You Think You Can Do That

People who aspire to be managers often assume they can readily perform the duties of that position. If truth be told, you often think you can do your boss's job. However, beware of the many behind-the-scenes, often hidden, or invisible managerial tasks for which your supervisor is responsible, but of which you might not be aware. The complex nature of managerial duties is often invisible to the eyes of employees. If you set your sights on becoming a manager, take your time and first master the skills required to perform the present job successfully. Sometimes a great headwaiter makes for a lousy supervisor or manager. Sometimes a great front office manager makes for a good director of rooms. Rising from one job level to another involves new experiences, more employee responsibilities, and new task requirements that have yet to be learned. Judging someone's job duties from a distance is easy; however, if you make it to that next level, you should be aware that other people will suddenly judge you, too. If you seek to advance to the next level, educate yourself about all that the job entails and prepare accordingly.

Career Tip: The grass always looks greener on the other side. Only venture there if you really feel that you can do a good job. If you are promoted, concentrate on the job-skill and people-skill requirements of the new position. Once you are established in your new job and familiarize yourself with your new work environment, you can begin to try to improve it, strengthen your team or product, and work towards advancing your career.

22 Old Hogs

Dealing with an older supervisor is actually simple. Be quiet, watch, and learn. Older employees are usually fountains of knowledge and can have positive influences over the life progression and career paths of a young professional. Of course, there are exceptions, but in most cases, the mature mentor means well and aims to fill up your knowledge tank. Naturally, some of their methods might seem a little old-fashioned and more obscure to a younger employee who might not immediately understand or recognize the wisdom in them.

Career Tip: Never take things personally in your working life. Training, counseling, and guidance always aim to make you better and stronger. If a supervisor tries to get a point across to you and unexpectedly hurts your feelings, try to address it, directly, with that person. Most likely, the supervisor did not mean to hurt your feelings and, after a short discussion, any misunderstandings can be quickly settled.

---

23 Know Your Place

Building up over weeks, the day finally came, the day when the most important (past or present) head of state would be at the hotel. Everything was ready for this quick and confidential lunch meeting. My superior happened to be a woman and while I organized everything for the big day, she was still the mastermind shadowing us all. On the actual day, the news came that the head of state would now be arriving at a different entrance than planned with his entourage and security. Ok, no big deal! We were ready no matter what entrance he wished to use. However, 45 minutes before the actual arrival, my then boss was still not there so I gauged my distance to her office, travel speed, and return time and then headed to her office.

I was very nervous and she was still sitting behind her desk as if nothing special was to happen shortly. I said, "The VIP is about to arrive in 30 and it's time to make our way down."

She calmly looked me in the eye and said, "You go and handle it."

I was perplexed and was about to ask for her reasons but, knowing her, I understood that she had given me "the look," which, in this case, was an executive order. So I closed my mouth and went back to the arrival point. Lots of cars, heavy security, and the entourage came. I welcomed and escorted them inside the building.

Shortly before we arrived at the lunch meeting venue, she was there, gracefully welcoming them, extending her hand to the head of state, and wishing all the guests a pleasant lunch. I spent the next three hours ensuring that the meeting and lunch were executed to perfection, and then I escorted the heads of state back to their departure points. Again, she was there to bid them all farewell.

Now it was my time. Filled with curiosity, I went to her office and questioned her motives and actions. She was number one and I was her second in command so it just did not compute for me. I asked why she had not been there upon arrival at the driveway. She asked me to sit down and then she started to elaborate.

The bottom line was that the change of entrance had a glitch with respect to diplomatic protocol. That particular entrance had an elevator to the lunch venue and had she been present, the head of state would have had no choice but to offer for her to go into the elevator first. According to diplomatic protocol, this would have been wrong. Thus, she opted to avoid that situation altogether and instead greet the head of state at the entrance of the lunch venue. While her decision had not made sense to me earlier, it now did.

What a smart and educated lady she was! To date, I still think that she was one of the most important mentors in my life.

24 IQ and EQ

Intelligence Quotient (IQ) and Emotional Intelligence (EQ) are both important for things to consider when working in the hospitality industry. The industry relies on an infinite number of customer-related interactions, and individuals with a low EQ often have difficulty sensing the special needs of a guest or a staff member. When IQ and EQ are combined, they provide a strong foundation for making the right customer- and employee-related decisions for any situation.

Career Tip: If you possess both a high IQ and a high EQ, you are perfect for the luxury hospitality industry. This industry is a people-oriented business and it needs individuals who possess both qualities. If you are deficient in one or the other, it is possible to acquire, and fine-tune, IQ and EQ over time. To learn more about your personal IQ and EQ capabilities, check with your company's human resources department. Many companies hire consulting firms to test staff IQ and EQ levels. You can also find multiple-choice questionnaires relating to IQ and EQ capabilities on the Internet. Since more of these online IQ and EQ tests provide just a sampling of the longer, more complex tests administered by professionals, their accuracy may not be as good. Still, you might find it an interesting exercise and a preliminary way to gain a sense of your own IQ and EQ levels.

25 Memory Vault

The information stored in your personal memory will become more and more important as you advance in your career. Some simple ways to fill your memory storage bank include asking questions and not pretending to know the answers if you do not know them. You can also use your eyes to fuel your curiosity. At those times when you ask a question and do not receive an answer, ask someone else or do some research until your appetite for this particular topic is satisfied. The complexity of a profession gets harder and harder as the years progress and, thus, your questions will never end.

Career Tip: Knowledge is king. The sooner that you recognize and accept this fact, the more quickly you will begin to seek out the knowledge you need to succeed, and the more advanced you will be among your peers. Even if the knowledge you seek will not be of use to you until sometime in the future, one day life will catch up with you and the knowledge you gained in the past will be ready and waiting for you to use. So, keep seeking as much information as possible throughout your lifetime and throughout your professional career. However, be careful not to become a bluffer, pretending that you know something when you do not. Most often that approach leads to a "crash and burn" and a woeful decrease in your credibility and integrity.

26 Smiley Recipe

Walk and talk with a smile. While everyone has his or her share of challenges and problems, why worry about all the negative things in life while you are working? Your problems will still be there after your shift ends. While at work, focus on the task on hand and greet everyone in the front and back of the house with a smile. Do not worry if the smiles that you give are not always returned. Smiles have a way of being infectious. Eventually, people will smile in response to your cheerfulness. This smiley recipe applies to everyone; it is part of your uniform and should be used with guests, co-workers, suppliers, and everyone else in your immediate area of contact.

Career Tip: A smile radiates an extremely positive energy and is well perceived by everyone you meet. Any news or requests accompanied by a smile just feel so much better. Even in critical situations, a smile can calm people and turn a negative into a positive. Smile as often as you can. Smiles are free and they do not require much effort on your part.

27 When Mistakes Happen – Not the End of the Road

Mistakes can happen to anyone, from rank and file staff members to senior managers. If you happen to make a mistake, admit to it. While admitting to a mistake might momentarily take you out of your comfort zone, the discomfort will be short-lived. People who do not admit to their mistakes can carry the feeling of guilt for a long time and, in many cases, they will be exposed at one point or another anyway. A manager's mistakes can occur in the form of comments or statements that they make about a situation or a project that fails to work. A manager must also have the courage to say, "I was wrong." When a person admits to a mistake, the case is resolved and closed surprisingly quickly. Co-workers will be more willing to look you straight in the eye and respect your frankness. There might also be a time when a person, who knows about the apparent mistake you have made, questions you about it. Denying that you committed the mistake will not only place you in a bad light with that person, it will also harm your future creditability and reputation within the company. Living by the "straight-shooting guy" or "straight-shooting gal" code is a good thing.

Career Tip: Admitting to a mistake takes courage, but doing so has a positive effect on the recipients of your honesty or your apology. They will respect you for that, and respect is a very important component to any career. Of course, be careful not to make mistakes every day. Doing so can have an adverse effect on your career as well, even if you own up to the mistakes.

28 The Good Question Mark

There are times in everyone's professional life when they simply do not know something. What if that situation happens to you? The best route is to admit that you do not know and to ask for more information or to seek out the answer to the question. Oftentimes, people find themselves caught in a situation where a question is asked and the answer does not come naturally. Yes, this can be the result of a lack of knowledge or of being unprepared, but these issues can be overcome if you educate yourself on specific relevant topics and seek out the appropriate training needed to prepare yourself for an upcoming meeting or discussion. When interacting with a customer, if you find that you do not know the answer to a question that they pose, promptly seek the help of your peers and your managers because it is important to provide the customer with the answer he or she seeks without delay.

Career Tips: It is good and healthy to have questions. The more questions that you have, the better professional you will be if you seek out the answers instead of pretending to know something that you do not know. When you look for and find the right answers, you strengthen your ability to deliver a quality performance and satisfy your customers, whether those customers are your co-workers or guests. The same idea applies to people who have questions for you.

29 Reasonable Doubts

From time to time, an employee might question the abilities of his or her manager or supervisor. While there can be good reasons for doing so, it is important to remember that the person in question possesses certain abilities that placed him or her in the managerial role. Therefore, it is always advisable to adopt a short "wait and see" attitude and extend a grace period to the manager or supervisor. One never knows what the future will bring and maybe this manager will turn out to be a great leader. If not, do not leave your job because of a difficult situation with a manger or supervisor because you may find a similar scenario in the next work place. Make sure you choose your career path wisely.

Career Tip: At some point in your life, you will face a challenging situation regarding someone for whom you work. This is only natural. Be sure that you properly evaluate the situation before making a judgment and be certain that your work performance is as good as you think it is.

30 Looking Through That (Real) Glass

Unless windows are frosted or decorated, they are transparent in nature. While this statement seems obvious, some organizations should review this topic in their orientation and training programs. This is especially true for managers and staff that are working in the lobby, entrance, and restaurant areas of luxury hospitality facilities. How many times has a customer approached the hotel entrance with luggage and were assisted only after they had entered the doors? How many times has a guest been sitting on the terrace, watching the waiters in the restaurant through the window, while patiently waiting for service? These scenarios are annoying for guests and being subjected to them starts their experience off on the wrong note. A simple adjustment in the training manual, or the resetting of an area's parameters, could eliminate these issues and add a little extra-special, ever so valuable touch, to a customer's experience.

Career Tip: You will save yourself a lot of energy if you look through the window and prepare for whatever situation is before you or whatever situation that may eventually arise. These few, crucial seconds of looking into the distance can often determine your success with regard to a customer's first impressions of your company and his or first interactions with you.

31 Body Language Talks

Running or hurrying through public or operational areas to fulfill a guest's requests in the shortest possible time might seem like a good idea, but, unfortunately, as you scurry about, the eyes of all the other guests are upon you as well, and these guests may or may not fully understand the intention behind your urgency. Consequently, they may be unnecessarily alarmed by your actions. The same holds true for such actions as turning your back and pretending that no one can see you while scratching your head, looking at your watch while approaching a guest, or raising an eyebrow when speaking to a colleague with your face towards customers. Be aware: your actions will be seen by others.

Career Tip: Try to avoid inappropriate gestures or body language. Remember that, unless you are in an isolated office space, you are always "on stage" and people will always be able to observe you. Just because you cannot see the person behind you does not mean that person cannot see you. This is true even if you are standing at a distance from a customer or a guest. More often than not, any number of people will be able to observe your facial and body expressions.

32 The Unpolished Diamond

There was once an independent, famous chef during a time when franchising was just about to become popular. The general manager of a hotel summoned this chef, seeking to convert an existing hotel restaurant into a trendy eatery using that chef's name and menu. The general manager had all the plans in place and all the investors lined up. One of his culinary protégés was selected to head up this restaurant.

When this famous chef agreed to lend his name and concept to the enterprise, he also added a condition that surprised the general manager. The condition was that the famous chef would personally handpick the chef who would run the restaurant that would bear his name. When the search began, this famous chef visited all the existing kitchens of the hotel franchise and met with many potential cooks, each of whom aspired to be chosen for the special role.

In the end, this famous chef picked a person that nobody anticipated. The man he chose was an unknown chef who had been cutting vegetables in the banquet kitchen for several years. The chosen chef was introverted and had a medium-sized build and unkempt, shoulder length black hair. He was hardly the type of person that one would have expected this famous chef to select for this job.

The cook agreed and, despite objections, the general manager agreed as well. The cook was shipped off to the flagship restaurant located in the famous chef's country. There, the cook was put through a monstrous, extremely difficult three-month regime.

When this once-shy and introverted cook returned to head up the hotel franchise restaurant, people who knew him dropped their jaws. His physique had become athletic. He now sported a white-blond, spiked hairstyle and wore small, diamond earrings. Most of all, he talked like there was no tomorrow.

What is more, he cooked like a god and created a dream team for his kitchen. His culinary execution was flawless and measured up to the same perfection as the famous chef's flagship restaurant. His customer skills were stunning and the restaurant was extremely successful for years thereafter. The general manager was complimented for establishing such a profitable venue.

The moral of this story is that every employee is a good employee. Remember: there are plenty of hidden talents and diamonds in the rough among all employees.

SOME CAREER POINTERS

33 Looking at the Horizon – Journey of Life

Have you ever looked at the endless horizon and wondered what lies beyond? Something comes, that is for certain. The same idea applies to one's career. Something new always comes, even if we do not recognize it right now. It is important to focus your attention on the professional journey ahead of you. Make that next dream step a reality by dedicating your ambitions, efforts, and skills towards attaining that next point in your life.

Career Tip: Keep in mind that everything is possible and achievable as long as it is realistic and within the parameters of your abilities. Envy is cowardly whereas courage and ambition are positive ingredients for a successful life.

34 The Clock Is Ticking

A typical timetable for a professional life is as follows: ages 15-20 are your basic study years; ages 21-29 are your professional and academic experience years; ages 30-40 are your make it or break it years; ages 40-45 are your apply your knowledge years; and age 50 and above will be addressed in my next book, once I know more about that age range.

Career Tip: This career roster is meant to be a guideline and to serve as a general indicator. How one "packs and stacks" his or her efforts to rise faster depends entirely on the individual, but major career progression steps normally occur in 5- and 10-year cycles.

35 Professional GPS

In the very early stage of a career, it is always good to map out your career path aspirations. Based on your personal ambitions and beliefs, create a career ladder plan. Start with the position that you are currently in and sketch the stages of your intended progression and the positions that you hope to obtain over the next 5 to 10 years. Keep that piece of paper in a safe place. Every time you achieve a step on that career ladder, place a check mark by the goal and date it as well. A career map is useful to anyone. As this book will illustrate, everyone, from apprentice to CEO, needs a goal.

Career Tip: This career ladder can be a major motivator as you progress in your professional career ambitions. Checking off your goals as they are met adds new fuel and strength to your personal and professional goals. Attaining your goals earlier than you had anticipated increases your self-confidence as well.

36 Walking the Talk

Leading by example is a common phrase often used in any business; however, it actually takes a lot of self-discipline to walk the right path. The hotel industry provides many temptations and the higher that you rise in your career, the more temptations there will be. It is crucial to avoid these temptations and live by a code of respect and integrity at all times. The higher rank that you achieve within your company, the more eyes there will be upon you. These eyes will not only seek your knowledge and guidance, they will also judge you for your behavior and your personal conduct.

Career Tip: While guests will definitely observe you, so will your co-workers and others in your company. A solid performance and a flawless behavioral track record are equally crucial. Too many times, taking a wrong turn, with regard to personal conduct, can be the downfall of a person's career.

37 The Straightened Spine

Are your supervisors tough? Well, all of my supervisors were tough, but if I could turn back time, I would not change even one of them. Yes, there can be hard times and hardships, but one day you will look back and actually be very grateful to those people who brought out the best in you. You will learn from the good, and the not so good, supervisors. The good practices will become part of your professional future. The worst practices will be those that you will avoid and will not want to repeat during your career.

Career Tip: Tough mentors or superiors are blessings in disguise. Many times, they really can bring you to the brink of self-doubt, but if you can master their demands, you will become stronger. Doing so will also bring recognition and respect from your supervisors and, maybe, you might earn the special added tasks or the promotion for which you have been looking.

38 The Professional Toothbrush

What is quality? Textbooks say that quality is a system that measures customer satisfaction. I say quality is a habit. Close your eyes and imagine that you are in your bathroom at 3 AM. The lights are out and you have to reach for your toothbrush. In this situation, 99 out of 100 times, you will immediately find it because knowing where it is has become a habit. Anything else that you do over and over again can become a habit, too. Quality can become a habit if you train repeatedly and apply it to the best of your abilities.

Career Tip: Habits help you to perform something as repetitively and consistently as possible. Find the highest performance standard for a task and make it a habit. Soon you will be able to handle multiple tasks simultaneously, adding more high-level productivity to your work performance.

39 Perfection – The Chill Down Your Neck

What is perfection in the hospitality industry? Perfection is the total commitment to service excellence. This is exemplified by doing the things right, not only the first time, but every time with the eagerness and precision of a Swiss watchmaker. Perfection feels good and boosts self-esteem. Very often perfection does not go unnoticed by customers and peers alike. It is important to note, however, that perfectionist behavior should never be executed at the expense of customer convenience or create an adverse effect on your co-workers. Have you ever executed a function to its total perfection, for example, baked a cake or mixed a martini to its ultimate level? Have you ever serviced a customer in a timely and professional manner in such a way that no wish could have been left unfulfilled? There are as many scenarios as there are departments within the luxury hospitality industry, but if you are a person with a perfectionist passion, every company will hold you in high regard.

Career Tip: If you ask a Japanese master who is best in his field how to attain perfection, he will tell you that there is no perfection, only the continued attempt to make something better. Remember, even if you think that you are the best, there will always be something or someone who is better. Therefore, it is important to keep working and improving yourself all the time.

40 Knowledge Launch

Every trade has its own knowledge parameters and, in most cases, any additional knowledge must be acquired by one's own drive and initiative. Blaming your supervisor for not teaching you enough is one way to hide beneath the glass-ceiling barrier. Another commonly noted excuse is that one simply does not have enough time to obtain the additional knowledge required to excel in one's position. That excuse is only for the weak-minded. The go-getter will find time, and ways, to acquire the knowledge that will take him or her to the next level. If, for example, the labor laws are not against it and your boss does not mind, why not volunteer for a few hours in a different department after your regular shift is over? You can also dedicate some of your leisure time to visiting a bookstore or a library to catch up on the latest trends and advances in a particular area or to learn more about a specific topic. How far you will progress depends entirely on your aspirations and how much extra time that you are willing to invest in your future.

Career Tip: Always remember that if you point one finger at a person, three fingers will point back at you. That is how life is. Nothing is for free. It is always easier to blame another person rather than accept the blame yourself. That is why it is always better to concentrate on the person at whom the three fingers are pointing.

41 Getting Started in New Environments

In whatever position you find yourself, be sure to learn everything that you can about your new environment and your responsibilities, as fast as possible. Doing so will enable you to work in a way that brings the results you desire and will build trust between yourself and your supervisors and peers. Learn to enjoy unfamiliar territories, as these are the areas in which you can learn something new.

Career Tip: Any new environment can be challenging at first. Do not worry. You will soon get the hang of it and it will become part of your daily routine and a good habit. Trust in yourself, pay attention to what is being taught, and become familiar with your work environment. Familiarity breeds comfort and peace of mind, which will free up space for all the new things that you need to learn.

42 Staying the Course

Being a recognized asset to your company is attained only through your performance. If you consistently bring desired results or achieve your assigned goals, your company will hold you in high regard and, in most cases, promotions or added responsibilities will follow. Of course, there are those undeserving individuals who may slip through the cracks undetected; However, be aware, they will be caught someday, and their rising careers will come crashing down faster than when they rose to prominence.

Career Tip: Companies and managers like employees that perform well and consistently. Delivering a good performance gives your manger confidence in you and lets him or her concentrate on other things. They will also keep you at the top of their mind if some special project arises that requires your involvement.

43 Lateral Service

Help others. If you are really so good at your job that everything is perfect and under control, step outside your boundaries and assist your peers. Doing so will build goodwill and it will also serve as a good training ground for teamwork and integrity building. Lateral service can be applied across the field. All it takes is your own confidence.

Career Tip: Co-workers need help all the time. If you are able to spare the time and effort to help others, gratitude and respect will come in return.

44 Climbing the Career Ladder

Whatever you do, do it right and, most importantly, do not stop. If you fulfill only the necessary requirements, your career is already in slow motion. Excel in everything that you do (every supervisor and manager likes that!). Once you are a master of that particular job, ask, "What's next?" It is not called the career ladder for no reason. Step-by-step, you can rise to the next level of achievement. This rule applies to everyone — from beginners to masters.

Career Tip: In any workplace, you are always under constant observation — be it from guests or from management. Stay focused on your professional tasks and priorities because if well mastered, your manager and supervisors will further test you by assigning additional tasks or promoting you to higher positions due to your capabilities.

45 Courage - Stand Up for Your Staff

Courage is one of the most important trademarks of a leader. There is nothing more disheartening than a supervisor or a manager who does not stand up for his people. If you are a supervisor or manager and are the shepherd of your herd, protect them with all your means. Mistakes will happen and a manager is ultimately responsible for them. Blaming the individual or the team involved is a cowardly method and is not an attribute of a trustworthy leader. Managers must shield their employees and workers from the external attacks that can be demoralizing and unhelpful. A manager should take responsibility and accept the blame for the mistake. Thereafter, he should do his job through mentoring or retraining the individual who committed the mistake in order to make that person a better professional and avoid reoccurrence in the future.

Career Tip: Leaders are supposed to be shields. Those shields are here to guard the staff from any outside influences that could hamper their motivation or performance during a conflict or personal attack. If a shield is properly applied, the staff will feel a sense of security, as well as support, and, in turn, will try to do their very best.

46 Decision-making

Decision-making is one of the most important tools that you will need for the rest of your professional life. Nobody likes indecisive people. Thus, if you are the person on whom people can depend and they know that you are the person who can make things happen one way or the other, you are a decision-maker. Do not forget to read the section about knowledge, because chances are, if you do not know what you are doing, your decision-making process will come to a standstill as a result of your fear of failure.

Career Tip: The decision-making process will be one of the most important areas in your professional life. If no decisions are made, processes will slow down or come to a standstill. So make it a habit to keep that process going and to keep your peers and employees moving forward. Timing is also of importance; the faster that you can make decision, the faster things will move.

47 Do Not Burn Bridges

Building professional relationships throughout your career is important since you will never know when you will be working or dealing with that person again. Never burn your bridges when you leave a job, or do away with that business relationship when you change companies. The luxury hotel industry is comprised of a very small circle of peers, suppliers, and customers.

Career Tip: The more people that you get to know in this small circle of luxury hotel employees, owners, and companies, the better it will be for you. No Web-based networking tool or machine can replace that trustworthy face-to-face relationship.

48 The Volunteer Pyramid

A career is a pyramid that is made of many blocks. To achieve a solid foundation of knowledge at various levels, and within various fields, requires time and experience. Each year will add new blocks to that pyramid, which will become taller and taller. Throughout your career, volunteer regularly for special tasks and projects, as these will gain you additional career building blocks and speed up your career advancement process. It will also enrich your personal experience and strengthen your value to the organization.

Career Tip: Each company will have plenty of opportunities for which you can volunteer. Keep yourself informed about the available opportunities. If you feel up to it, do not be afraid to ask about becoming a volunteer. The experience will enrich your knowledge and your life, making you a better asset to your company and your profession.

49 Personal Grooming

Whether you are going for an employment interview or are heading to work, always dress professionally. As the saying goes, you can tell the character of a person by his shoes. If you are given a standard uniform from your company, then wear it. However, if the suit or suits are ones that you provide at your own expense, remember that clothes make the person. Since you will spend the majority of your career life in your professional garb, be sure to invest in some good quality shoes and outfits. The right suits will make you feel better and investing in a few pairs of solid, quality shoes can also help you fight unnecessary, work-related fatigue.

Career Tip: Unfortunately, people often judge others by what they wear. Thus, whatever your personal style is outside the workplace, dress for success within your workplace. In addition, stay fit and energized by wearing good footwear, as this industry requires you to be on your feet for many hours each day.

50 Effective Briefings

To execute effective meetings, set an agenda that prioritizes a list of things to do before adjourning to daily morning meetings and briefings. If you are in charge of a group of people who are about to be briefed, be sure that you know everything there is to know about yesterday, today, and tomorrow. If you also present this information without the assistance of written notes, you will earn the respect of your team and be viewed as an effective leader.

Career Tip: Confident speakers and presenters are admired and respected by many. They will not only gain the trust of their listeners, they will command attention when they speak.

51 No Time Warp, Please

The future is now so do not spend too much time in the past. If something happened, so be it. Fix it, get over it, and then move on, as quickly as possible. There is nothing more unproductive and disturbing than when managers are stuck in the past. Yes, all good things can come to an end, but this should not be at the expense of aspiring individuals. Whining about the good times gone by, or about what a great life you had some time ago, is not a topic of interest to your employees or co-workers. Those managers who feel that way must come to terms with the past and begin to look forward, because that is where the future is.

Career Tip: People do not like people who refer to their past or previous companies, such as "We used to do it like that." The "We" has now become the present and the "We" is now the team with whom you are currently working. If you keep making references to the past, people will quickly judge you and feel disconnected from you.

52 Forgetting One's Own Basics

Delegating new employee orientation to staff members who are not well versed in the interpretation of rules and regulations is one of the most common mistakes that a manager makes with new employees. In too many cases, managers have forgotten what they have learned over the years and from where they initially came before advancing through the ranks. Thus, newcomers are quickly assigned to the next capable person and, in most cases, the assignment of relating the rules and regulations is handed down and down until nobody lower is left to attend and train the newcomer. Hence, the first impressions of the newcomer, as well as the newcomer's initial skill-set training, will only be as good as the person who was assigned the task of orienting the new employee.

Career Tip: It is a grave mistake for a manager not to establish the first impression personally with a new employee. The consequence of that decision is that the correct interpretation of rules and regulations is spiraled down the delegation ladder to a staff member who is at a level in which he or she may not really know what the highest expectations are.

53 First Time General Managers

As with all professions and career levels, first-time general managers should work in luxury hotels that are smaller, sometimes in the same company's 4½ star category, than, or at least not as demanding as, the company's flagship properties. This will enable the new general manager to settle into his or her new position and give him or her, and the company, a chance to see how well the general manager performs his or her first full assignment of an asset or business unit. If the property is well managed and successful for the next two years, most companies will gladly move the new general manager to a more challenging and rewarding property.

Career Tip: First-timers will always be more observed than those who already have a proven track record. If a plate is loaded too full and too fast, the individual's performance could suffer and affect the business unit's results.

54 Swiss Time Management Principles

Never be late for meetings or anything else with a time-sensitive goal. Be professional and always arrive at a meeting or an appointment a few minutes early. Being late is unprofessional and disrespectful to others who were there on time. Being early also allows you to relax for a few minutes or prepare for the meeting.

Career Tip: People generally do not like latecomers. Regardless if you are a rank and file staff member or management, coming or showing up late creates a negative perception of you. This does matter, whether you are a waiter arriving late for a shift or the CEO who brings his management team to a standstill due to an unnecessary wait.

55 The Wrong Start to a Morning

Be prepared when attending meetings. There is nothing more annoying and disruptive when managers have not yet spoken to their staff or read the prior night's reports and, therefore, cannot answer the questions posed by their superiors or peers. Being unable to answer correctly and promptly will decrease their trust in you and raise questions about your capabilities and your ability to be responsible for areas, departments, or divisions.

Career Tip: Being prepared is something that should be on everybody's agenda at all times. If everyone is prepared, meetings can be conducted more quickly and more effectively, gaining that extra time to attend to other pressing tasks and responsibilities.

56 The Double Check

You have an idea and want to implement it. If you are confident that it will work, go ahead and do it. However, if the slightest doubt is present, prepare a small presentation and share it with your colleagues and peers or a selected group of outsiders. At the end of the presentation, invite questions and suggestions. This will not only improve your initial proposal, it will also increase your chances of being more successful.

Career Tip: Multiple brains are better than one — even when the person who spearheaded the entire project thinks otherwise. Testing and running an idea or project by others will safeguard the company from any unexpected failures and guarantee a better result or outcome.

57 Art of Stress - The Tight Timeframe

Stress is when you are placed into a timeframe that is no longer manageable. Sometimes you cause it yourself and sometimes it is caused by someone else.

Both scenarios are not comfortable and, depending on the situation, can result in anxiety and emotional distress. It is hard to determine how to avoid stress, but an open mindset and preparedness can often help one to avoid a stressful moment. If work or workloads become unmanageable, operational staff will become prone to mistakes and managers will face the burnout factor of prolonged working hours.

Career Tip: Do not think that working into the late evening hours every day makes you a better employee. There are some old-fashioned managers that want you to do just that, but it is more likely that senior management frequently passing by your desk will question your abilities in the current job, think that you may be overloaded, and question whether you can properly manage the tasks. To avoid pressure-cooker scenarios, look ahead and try to predict upcoming deadlines and volumes that need your extra effort and readiness.

58 Pursuing That Idea

Do not be discouraged if you have an idea and nobody shares your excitement right away. Work on it any way and, if it is successful, everyone who questioned you or did not initially believe in you will suddenly become your friends and best pals. The bottom line is that you are the one who will feel good in the morning.

Career Tip: People with ideas, and the will to pursuit those ideas, are respected and admired by many. This is especially true if the idea improves the work environment and affects customer service or company returns in a positive way. Chances are that your company will hold you in high regard and reward you accordingly.

59 Global Village

With the world becoming a global village and people from all nations and ethnic backgrounds migrating to major cities around the world, the cultural sensitivity of each guest or co-worker must be respected at all times. Whether in reference to a guest or a subordinate, the customer service person or manager must be able to understand the different needs of individuals and react accordingly. It must also be understood that in today's age of global transportation, people have travelled to many different corners of the world and are well aware of how a true burger, pizza, sushi, or shepherd's pie should taste.

Career Tip: The world is already an international playing field and this means that, one day or another, you will work with people from different countries and ethnic backgrounds. It is important to respect that and not let personal beliefs encumber your professional relationships.

60 Managing Complacency

Many times an individual who has been assigned to repeated tasks becomes complacent. What happened to that very nice frontline staff member who suddenly lost her sparkle and shiny appearance or that energetic recreation guy who no longer seems to be charged up? In most cases, these individuals have been left to do their jobs with little or no feedback or attention for too long. They have no one to motivate them so they begin to do their job mechanically and nothing else. Nothing is sadder than to see than a once-passionate employee who, months later, becomes someone with little or no visible energy or enthusiasm for his or her work. People must be constantly nurtured and monitored; otherwise, even the brightest stars can lose their shine.

Career Tip: Every person has his or her own bright personality. In a workplace, that personality can go into hiding if one does not feel cared for, or worthy of, the work performed. A tap on the shoulder, a simple "Thank you" or "Good job, well done" can do miracles and help these employees keep their heads high at all times.

61 Professional Fear

Fear of the unknown is good, at least when it comes to one's professional life. The tingling sensation in the stomach is a sign of unknown things to come or, sometimes, the fear of confrontation if someone is unprepared for a situation. If the tingling sensation is related to the unknown, remember it will be soon gone and the task on hand will become a habit and part of your experience, making you a more thorough and competent professional.

Career Tip: Challenge yourself to go after new things, even if they seem unreachable at the beginning. Your supervisors will treasure your courage and think highly of you if you take on uncharted territories and tasks.

62 Being Taken Advantage Of

There will always be people who take advantage of other people. Good-willing and talented individuals often fall prey to people who are skilled at taking advantage of others or who, because it is more convenient, prefer to have others accomplish tasks that they could easily do for themselves. If someone asks you for a favor, there is no harm in lending a helping hand once in a while. If the favors are never returned or if they affect your personal job performance, you may want to analyze the favors that you hand out before you agree to give them. Saying no, once in a while, will quickly expose the character of the person asking for assistance. If the person is understanding and still treats you the same, then continue to help occasionally. If that person loses their temper quickly and gives you an irritated or angry look, you may wish to remove that individual from your "freebie list."

Career Tip: Do not be afraid to say "No" occasionally and sort out the "I want to help" from the "I don't want to help" recipients of your efforts.

63 Odd Tasks That Stick Forever

As you progress in your professional life, there will be those odd tasks that you will be asked to perform. These can range from polishing the cutlery to making up a bed or cleaning a toilet. While these may not be the most desired of duties, be aware that they are essential experiences that will enhance your working knowledge later in your career.

Career Tip: No matter what tasks you are assigned during the progression of your career, you should always remember that these tasks will add another level of knowledge to your skill-set. This knowledge will become essential down the road when the time has come for you to be in charge. This knowledge will enable you to conduct proper inspections and will also give you the ability to show people how the task should be done in the first place. This will make you a respected and effective leader.

64 Equal Treatments - Respect

The "treat everyone equally" rule applies to all. The doorman should treat the arriving cab driver with respect, the receiving officer should do the same to the arriving supplier, and so forth. If you do not take this rule to heart, you will unintentionally trigger an intangible consequence. For example, consequences can take the form of the cab driver who no longer puts your company's name at the forefront when being asked "Who's the best in town?" on the drive in from the airport, or suppliers who no longer want to uphold their quality guarantee to you, due to the disrespectful treatment that they received when serving you.

Career Tip: Always put yourself into another person's shoes and remember to treat everyone the way you wish to be treated. You are also the representative of your company; therefore, keep in mind that your behavior — whether positive or negative — will automatically reflect upon the image of the company for which you are working.

65 Forward Thinkers

While working for a company, perform your job to the best of your abilities. If you feel that you are on par and have a little free time on your hands, focus on your future and spend time learning about the other departments and products of your company. Firstly, you may be surprised at how various things that you did not know about are connected to one another and, secondly, you may discover how many of these things are actually taken for granted even though they involve a great deal of work and expertise. Finding out about all of these "nuts and bolts" will help you to be more efficient and effective in your workplace.

Career Tip: In the early stages of your career, and in the later stages as well, it is always good to show an interest in things beyond your immediate areas of responsibility. Adding more knowledge by learning the ins and outs of a company will help you progress faster and make you a more qualified person when the company, or your supervisors, need a helping hand.

66 Creativity Block

If you are in charge of a thriving department or division that constantly seeks new innovations and ideas, one day you might experience a creativity block. Do not be concerned. Many other people experience creativity blocks, and many other types of blocks, throughout the course of their lives. Your creativity block may mean that you have momentarily exhausted your creativity tank. You must, and then find ways to refill it. There are many different ways to do this. Some people find it helpful to read magazines or watch movies or documentaries. Others simply find that taking the time to rest their mind can help them overcome that momentary blockage. People are also creative at different times of the day. Some are highly creative in the shower while some need the tranquil silence of a night on their home's patio. Being creative at work can also present a challenge due to the many interruptions that one encounters during the course of the day.

Career Tip: Creativity will become an important part of your career. As you rise in the ranks, you will be required to contribute more often to a variety of levels and situations. Try to be creative every day and spend a few minutes, or more, on generating a variety of ideas. Even if you just pencil it down and keep it somewhere, the daily routine of challenging your mind will keep you sharp.

67 Copy Cats – 99.9%

Remember, if you copy something it will never be better than the original. If you have exhausted all your ideas, but still have nothing new or original to show for your efforts, analyze the matter again and then brainstorm by yourself or with others. The ideal scenario would be to reinvent the idea, transform it so that it becomes better than the original. Also, be aware that if you invent something new, other copycats will follow your lead. Thus, update your idea frequently to stay ahead of your competition or, even better, periodically generate some new ideas.

Career Tip: All ideas and products need to be reengineered or reinvented at one time or another. This applies to your business, as well. If you do not improve your business or your products, at some point, your competition might gain the upper hand and offer better or more updated products. Even the intangible world of the hospitality industry needs to be updated.

68 Thinking Outside the Box

If you are ever reprimanded by a manager for not thinking outside the box, simply ask for a specific example of how this manifests in your behavior. Oftentimes, the manager will not be able to provide you with a specific answer. If your manager is able, you are in good hands. The ability to think outside the box comes from experience and is not an easy thing for young individuals, who are just starting in the industry, to accomplish. Of course, there are exceptions and, sometimes, there are very creative young minds among us. To think outside the box for a particular topic, write your idea in the center of the page and then start scribbling anything that comes to mind. Stray as far as you can and do not let borders restrain the flow of your creativity. You may be surprised at how often the results can be remarkable. Thinking inside the box is doing something the way it has always been done or the ways it has always been required to be done. Thinking outside the box is asking for new ways of doing something. It creates multiple, innovative ideas that can create improvements and edgy results.

Career Tip: Depending on your career, life and work will challenge you periodically and, perhaps, even more often than you would expect. It is important to keep your mind challenged all the time by thinking up new ideas and new ways of doing things. If you have a glimmer of an idea about something in the middle of the day, do not lose it. Simply pencil it down and keep it somewhere, where you can find it later. You never know when you may need to draw on some previous thoughts or ideas.

69 Success Attributes

Precision, perfection, attention to detail, and zero defects are all attributes that make a successful individual. If you start with this mindset in the early part of your career, you will embark on a good path. These attributes must be applied, as often as possible, to every aspect of your career, no matter how small or big the item or task seems at the time. If all of the above attributes work for you, pay special attention to zero defects. Zero defects will help keep the road ahead of you clear and enable you to move forward.

Career Tip: Companies and managers are always on the lookout for that special person. If your attributes are aligned, you stand a pretty good chance of being chosen to take that next big step, position, or project. If management entrusts you to perform an upcoming task and you fulfill those expectations, more tasks will follow and your superiors will gain more confidence in your abilities.

70 Rewarding Tiredness

In theory, a creative and aspiring top manager is someone who never sleeps, or so some would lead you to believe. He or she has a personality that constantly thinks about new ways and procedures to improve the business and the well-being of the staff. This can be tiring, but it also can be the most rewarding time of your professional life. If you have the energy and can do it, go for it. You can sleep the additional hours later.

Career Tip: A career can be exhausting as you invest a lot of time creating and growing it. Rest assured that your body and mind will get used to the daily physical and mental challenges. Still it is important to find a fine balance between work and rest.

---

71 The Burnout Factor

Burnout can be self-inflicted or inflicted by someone else. A person experiences burnout when the body and mind have reached their maximum capabilities. When unmanageable workloads do not lessen or short-staffed offices handle business beyond their capabilities and no one comes to the rescue, burnout can kick-in. Consequently, the staff either quits or loses engine power (similar to a car that has run out of gas). Regardless of how burnout happens, in most all cases, both the business and the working environment suffer until the issues have been addressed and dealt with reasonably.

Career Tip: If one feels close to burning out, it is important to find ways to take a break and recharge. If one is responsible for people who are about to burnout, the same holds true. It is important to identify and understand your limits and the limits of your team. If priorities need to be shifted or schedules need to be reviewed, it is up to you to make that happen.

---

72 Light Bulb Story

One day a general manager came and pointed out the dusty light bulbs on a restaurant's numerous ceiling chandeliers. The respective manager called housekeeping to handle the job and the case was closed. The next day, the general manager visited once more and again pointed out that the light bulbs were still dusty. The respective manager was apologetic and promised that the chandeliers would be cleaned immediately.

The respective manager called housekeeping once again, emphasizing that the general manager was unhappy and, so, he thought the case was closed. On the third day, the light bulbs were still dusty. The general manager summoned the respective manager and harshly reprimanded him. While the manager tried to place blame on housekeeping and drum up many other reasons, the general manager taught him a very important lesson. Being a manager meant that he had to take responsibility for everything in his area.

The respective manager was unable to get the required assistance from housekeeping on that day due to a staff shortage. Being afraid of another lecture from the general manager, he decided to clean all the light bulbs on his own, by hand, in between breaks and late into the night. The next morning, the respective manager felt that he deserved recognition or a thank you for a job well done.

The general manager came, walked around, and headed towards the exit without a saying word. He suddenly stopped and flagged the manager. The manager, hoping for that recognition, rushed towards the general manager, who questioned, "You see that planter?"

The respective manager replied, "Yes."

The general manager asked, "Do you see that plastic underliner?"

The respective manager again answered, "Yes."

The general manager said, ""It's dusty!" and then he departed.

The manager felt a deep disappointment, but he also felt a great urge to always be a step ahead of his superiors from there on out. To this date, that attitude has served him well and this hardheaded mentor stays true to his heart.

THAT GUEST OF YOURS

73 Where Do Experiences Start?

How does one create that 100% customer experience and when does the experience for the customer actually start? If I leave my house to go on a business trip or fly somewhere on vacation, my experience will begin right at my doorstep and will not end until I return home. All the stories that I tell my friends and family will be about the trip from A to Z. But in the hotel industry, do we consider that? Not really, or at least not very often. For most reservations, flight information is available, including information about the destination from which the plane had just come and where it touched down at 2 AM that morning. Therefore, it would be very helpful if one were especially sensitive to those guests who just had a long and tiring flight. They have only one thing in mind: a warm welcome with a fast check-in. They also wish to continue the fabulous service experience they had in that wonderful business class or first class cabin.

Career Tip: It is important to predict the origin of your customers. If you manage to judge it correctly and treat them accordingly, you will improve your chances of success with regard to setting a positive and enjoyable first impression. Build yourself a scenario chest for a variety of customer experiences and try to apply these principles each time a customer walks through the door. A customer could be coming off a flight, could have just arrived by car, or could have simply walked in off the street. Still, it is important to remember that each of them had a starting point, somewhere.

74 Nothing Left to Chance

One of America's top chefs was not only in town but was also staying at the hotel. He was attending an upcoming special gala dinner for 70 invited guests for whom he would be cooking. The hotel's food and beverage teams were excited and on top of the VIP guest chef's demanding requests; preparations were in full gear.

Knowing the top chef's reputation and extremely high standard for excellence, there was only one problem — I was the only one who could execute his dinner, but I was also 8,850 miles away at a sales conference where I had been for the past four days. So, what to do? I decided that in the best interest of the teams and the dinner, I would cut my business trip short by a day and fly back in time. So I finished the last business appointment of the day, rushed to the airport, changed planes twice, and in no time (well, 28 hours!) I was back in town, merely four hours before the dinner.

Meanwhile, while I was in the air, the top chef decided to change the menu to accommodate 70 guests, thereby, making it a bit more challenging for his team and mine. He decided that the menu for the female guests should be different from that of the male guests. There was now a seven-course menu with 14 dishes (7 each) to be served to 70 guests within less than three hours. No problem! An army of hotel chefs, helpers, and waiters was on standby to assist with the execution of the night's event, so there were no concerns.

I then asked my director, who was in charge of the event, how he was planning to serve female dishes and male dishes without causing the wait staff confusion. I received a blank stare and, most importantly, no answer. Naturally, the situation — having received no answer, coupled with the fear of causing confusion during service — instantly made my brain rattle. Suddenly, the proverbial light bulb appeared and there was my answer — white gloves! White gloves were the answer!

I immediately summoned my head housekeeper to request white gloves for 30 waiters and sent my PA to the office to get me a green and a red marker. Once I had both, the solution was quite simple. Instead of challenging the part-time wait staff to remember each guest, we assigned each of them to two precise seats at two tables. Once they knew their seats, all we had to do was wait for the guests to be seated.

After the guests were seated, the director in charge of the event had the task of indicating on a pre-drawn floor and seating chart which chair was occupied by a male or female guest. As soon as the list arrived, I sent for the wait staff, lined them up in a pre-arranged order, and asked them to hold out their hands. What followed were the white gloves. I took the list and, based on the seating information, marked the bottom of the white gloves with red circles and green crosses; red represented male and green female.

Then, the dinner began and I retreated to the kitchen where the top chef awaited the signal to fire (a culinary term for start) his dinner. This process of preparing each plate from scratch is called dishing out and watching the top chef at work was pure enjoyment. His passion and precision, leaving nothing to chance, were wonderful. The food looked gorgeous, was full of textures and flavors, and, most importantly, was ready to be served to the guests.

Two chef lines were working on the dishes, one for the males and one for females. At the end of the line, the top chef would personally inspect every single plate before giving it to me. Behind me was also a long line of wait staff who were now waiting to come in and pick up the dishes. Five at a time, they reached out with their hands and showed me the colored markings on their white gloves. This way, each hand got the correct plate for the correct seat and all 70 guests with their 14 dishes had an exceptional experience.

The end of the night brought not only cheers from the dinner guests to the visiting top chef and his team, but also to all the employees of the hotel who had worked so hard to make the evening a memorable one.

75 Imperative Guest Focus

If you are in an environment in which customer service is crucial, focusing on the guest is imperative. Do not worry about impressing your manager; if all the guests are happy, your supervisor and the company's management will recognize that in due time. After all, people like to be surrounded with people who make them look good. Try to keep your eyes open to help as many guests as possible. This will assist you in applying your efforts in the right place and at the right time.

Career Tip: Doing your job well will result in customer satisfaction, which in turn will bring back customers and improve business. The better that you are with your guests, the more you free your manager to concentrate on his or her real duties. He or she will be grateful for their well-performing staff. The more focused that you are on your work, the easier it will be for you to deal with multiple guests at the same time.

76 Profiling

Customer profiling is a key aspect to positive customer service. Profile the person, or persons, coming towards you. Depending on the distance, you will have 5, 10, or 20 seconds, or more, to determine the demeanor, and sometimes even the personality, of the person(s) approaching you. If the person rushes into the lobby, chances are he or she is in a hurry and, thus, has little time or little patience for lengthy chitchat or for slow customer interaction. Speed is what the person needs, and, if fulfilled properly, meeting this need will result in a positive customer service experience for the customer. There is always a correct recipe for customer service success whether the customers stroll in, look fatigued, have children with them, or are beaming and lovey-dovey honeymooners.

Career Tip: Why is customer profiling important? It will help you to be better prepared to address the specific needs of the approaching customer(s). Profiling relies on your ability to use your eyes to assess a situation and your good judgment in predicting the needs of an upcoming customer. If you hit a high note with them, satisfaction is guaranteed.

77 Eyes and Ears

Your eyes and ears, as well as a good amount of common sense, are some of the most important tools at your disposal when dealing with customers and peers. These tools can also be helpful in most any scenario. Use your eyes to see what is coming at you and use the time to profile or make a judgment until you interact with your customer. Once you are in close contact, use your ears to listen very carefully and precisely for what the customer is requesting or saying. Do not let your mind wander away while a conversation is in progress and do not think that you already know, in advance, what the customer is going to say. This is a common mistake and wrong assumptions can often become the downfall of a situation.

Career Tip: People get irritated if they say or request something and then do not receive 100% satisfaction. It is important to listen carefully, repeat if necessary, and deliver 100% on your promises. Looking someone in the eye, reading his or her facial expressions, and listening carefully is not rocket science; it is just a matter of personal care.

78 Escorting Customers

Escorting guests is not a simple matter. Too many times the escort is impersonal, too fast for the guest's pace, or makes the guest feel like a number rather than a welcomed patron. If you do escort customers, do not make these mistakes. Take a moment or two to profile your guests. Thereafter, engage them in light conversation, if you feel they might enjoy that, and be attentive to their children. With these actions, you will be off to a good start.

Career Tip: Escorting customers takes skill. It involves more than just walking with someone. Once the customer steps through the hotel doors, an escort is part

THAT GUEST OF YOURS ■ 43

of their experience. Guests arrive at your hotel with preconceived expectations about your facility and they seek genuinely personalized service.

79 General Rules No Longer Apply

Whom to greet first used to be as simple as applying the "ladies first" rule. Today, customer recognition dynamics have changed. My new rule says that, if you are a woman, greet the female guest first and then the male guest. If you are a man, greet the male guest first and then the female guest. The last thing a guest needs is to have a young, good-looking male receptionist flirt with his wife before he even gets to the counter. The same rule applies to people with children. A guest's children are very important to them so why not acknowledge the kids first? When the kids are happy, the parents will be happy. In addition, remember that these children are potential, future guests.

Career Tip: Make sure that you know and understand your company's standards. With this knowledge in hand, do not hesitate to bend the rules a little here or there if doing so leads to better customer satisfaction. In restaurant environments, it is still important to serve the ladies first.

80 Eye Contact

Eye contact is probably one of the most important tools in customer service. Eye contact does not stop with the person standing right in front of you. There is nothing more annoying for customers, who happen to be in a long line or at the end of the line, than when the person behind the counter or podium is blindsided and fails to make eye contact. If you are the person behind the desk or podium, always remember to scan the line and nod or gently smile at every person who is waiting. It makes the guests feel good to be acknowledged and it takes a lot of pressure off you and your customers.

Career Tip: Looking into the eyes of a person is a sign of respect. If you do not make eye contact, the customer will perceive you as arrogant or not interested in their business. It is also important to choose the guest with whom you will make the first eye contact. If you are a female, first make eye contact with a female guest if she is arriving with her male partner. If you are male, the opposite applies. Eye contact is all about respect. Failure to make proper eye contact, even if you are with friends, is a sign of disrespect.

81 The Confidence Factor

This confidence factor rule applies to everyone in the luxury hospitality industry, but it is especially pertinent for restaurant and bar staff. A thorough knowledge of product offerings will instill personal confidence in the employee, which will then improve rapport with the customers. A solid knowledge base about the products that are offered makes you a more approachable person, as well as a better salesperson. With knowledge in hand and a good sense of how to profile your customers, chances are that you will anticipate your customer's wishes and also sell that extra menu or bar item. Additionally, your supervisor and your company will think highly of your performance and your abilities as you contribute positively to their bottom-line profits and customer satisfaction ratings.

Career Tip: While it may seem difficult to memorize the entire product line, it is important to do so. Try to learn about them in stages. Soon you will realize that it may not be as overwhelming as you had thought and you will suddenly gain a knowledge edge over others. Customers also appreciate wait staff and bartenders who are well versed in the restaurant and bar's complete line of offerings and provide service that goes beyond just suggesting the specials of the day.

82 Missing the Old Guards – The Maturity Pill

Mature concierges and restaurant managers are a valuable asset to any luxury hospitality facility. But, where have they all gone? At one time, patrons could ask the concierge a question and get a rapid, straight, and precise answer that suited their needs. The manager would smile and call you by name as he or she greeted you because you and your family had been patronizing that restaurant for generations and he or she knew you when you were a child. Sadly, this type of impeccable service is a thing of the past and a rare find in these days. Unfortunately, too many concierges have retired without being replaced or have been laid off and their departure has diminished that extra comfort-level for customers.

Career Tip: The "old guards," such as a seasoned concierge, provide an additional perception of quality in the minds of customers. These invaluable employees used to know everything there was to know about their business. Of course, this took years of learning, years of employment stability working in the same position or the same department, and an evolving knowledge base. Customer service is still an environment that requires a lot of face-to-face interaction and knowledgeable answers delivered, in person, by a human being rather than a website on the Internet. Young employees no longer have such finely tuned customer service skills or the desire to spend year after year in the same department or position. Thus, they quickly try to digest the departmental information that they think they need in order to answer customer questions without actually mastering the art of customer service.

83 Name Recognition

Name recognition is a cornerstone of superior customer service. While nobody expects an employee to memorize the names on all 50-250 reservations for that night, the cheat sheet, with the customer's name, that the hostess so nicely placed in your station or a quick look at the credit card when the bill is being paid can provide you with easy tools to say those magic words: "Thank you, Mr. Smith. Please come back again." The same principle applies to every aspect of the luxury hotel, restaurant, and bar industry. The majority of staff has access to digital displays on their phones, the receptionist has the pre-booking form, and the porter may be able to read the name of the luggage label. As the old saying goes, "Where there is a will, there is a way." There are many ways to learn a customer's name so there are really no excuses for not using name recognition as a customer service tool.

Career Tip: Customers appreciate it when people in the service industry recognize their names. This is an old expectation that will never fade. Guests like to be recognized by their names since it gives them a welcoming sense of belonging. Some employees find it easy to remember faces and names; others do not. Those who have a harder time remembering can utilize other ways to jostle their memories, such as striking up a short conversation with the customer or trying to identify something particular about that guest. If the customer leaves a $100 tip/gratuity, I am confident that he or she will be remembered for a long time. However, in a genuine customer service environment, a customer should not have to "pay" for name recognition.

84 Know Your Customers

A good understanding of customer demographics, a solid understanding of market trends, and keen insight into what your competition is offering (market intelligence) are essential key components in creating successful sales initiatives. Once all this information is gathered, sorted, and analyzed, you can develop strategies that will build the foundation of good customer initiatives.

Career Tip: Many mistakes or failed initiatives are often due to an error in focus. While it may be a good idea to focus your entire energy on the product you are about to create, if you do not place yourself into the shoes of your target audience, you may be in for a nasty surprise: no one may want what you are selling. Even if you successfully vie with your competition, a little effort in the market intelligence arena can result in increased business opportunities.

85 Responding in Time

Response time principles are simple. Nobody likes to wait too long for an answer or a request. In today's fast-paced world, time is money and if customers do not instantly receive the product information or answers that they need, they will go to a competing company and business will be lost. Therefore, make it a rule to respond immediately to face-to-face requests and to answer phone, e-mail, or other written forms within the time guidelines provided by your company if not faster. For requests from your supervisors, the same sense of urgency applies.

Career Tip: In the old days, a single product may have given you an edge over your competitors. In today's world, a single product will not suffice. If you do not take care of your customer's requests instantly, they will choose another company. Your competition may be in the same situation as you and has to deliver an answer, as fast as possible, to their clients; thus, if you let customers wait, they will have no other choice than to seek alternate answers elsewhere.

86 Timed Promises

When you promise to deliver a response or a product within a specific time frame, it is important to follow through. This is a very sensitive issue so do not overstate your ability to deliver as promised if you are not clear on how long it will take you to do so. Being late will irritate your customers and get them unnecessarily upset. Use your best judgment; if you really do not know how long it will take to fulfill a request, ask your supervisor and then provide the customer with a time frame that provides you with some wiggle room. For example, if your supervisor says that it will take two to three hours to fulfill a customer's request, tell the customer it will take three hours. If you are able to get back to them within two hours, the customer will be especially pleased because you were able to respond more quickly than anticipated. Of course, the goal should always be to deliver a request sooner rather than later, but in the worst-case scenario, make every attempt to deliver right at the stated time. Doing so will help you avoid any conflicts and uphold the customer's good faith in your company.

Career Tip: If you are new to a company, it will be difficult to judge perfect timing right away, but if you trust in the ability of your immediate co-workers and the staff in the other departments, promise within the time frame in which you think they can deliver. If you do not, you open yourself up to the possibility of creating a dissatisfied customer. Never blame the customer if you lose a deal. Put yourself in the customer's position and see if you would have been more tolerant than he or she was under the same circumstances. Most likely, the answer is that you probably would not have been.

---

87 Can or Cannot

The can-do attitude has a very positive effect on a customer's experience. However, too often companies unknowingly fall short in this area. Many customers will not say anything and simply do not return. If your customer return ratios dip, X-ray your operations and take a deep and serious look at them.

Restaurants and front desk operations are the epicenters of these situations. Consider the chef in the kitchen who refuses to honor the waiter's request to fulfill a guest's special order, only to see a manager override the chef in order to satisfy the guest. Think about the guest at check-in asking for a particular room preference and being declined because the request was not indicated on the reservation confirmation slip or in the hotel's computer system. In this situation, the manager comes to the rescue and provides the guest with the room of his or her choice. While the chef's response to the waiter might have been an example of one employee bullying another, the hotel reservation example could be simply due to the employee's lack of knowledge with regard to room inventory, availability, and allowable changes. Topics like these should be added to a company's training manual. Doing so would enable the staff to do a better job, and it would eliminate unnecessary wait time and annoyance for customers.

Career Tip: Customers do not want hear a reply that contains the word "cannot." If at all possible, offer an alternative that approximates the original request.

However, be cautious with regard to the insisting customer. They can usually get what they want by summoning your manager or whoever is the highest-ranking person working that day. It is advisable to avoid the need to involve your supervisor in order to resolve a customer service related concern. Think twice before saying no to a customer. Do not assume that the guest will let you, or your company, get away with shoddy customer service. The customer may check-in without receiving the room preferences they requested or eat the food they ordered without the extra changes they preferred, but beware that they may never return. This is known as an intangible loss, something you will never see and over which you will never have control.

88 Repeat Customers

One cannot over-state the importance of repeat customers. The topic of repeat customers has been trained, discussed, and repeated. However, each day, so many businesses lose valuable repeat customers due to negligence or complacency. Customer loyalty is such a big industry buzzword, but it is only applicable as long as nothing goes wrong. Replacing loyal customers will cost the company or a business a lot of time and more money.

Career Tip: Repeat customers are existing clientele. They are the backbone of any successful business. Customer loyalty and repeat business decreases the amount of time and money a company needs to spend in order to foster patronage and build a client base. If all goes well, existing customers will be your free ambassadors and generate new business for you due to their positive word of mouth. That is why losing loyal customers can be very costly to your employer and, ultimately, reduce your bonus or benefits at the end of the year. The extra money that might have been spent on employee benefits would have to be diverted into the company's marketing budget.

89 First and Last Contact

First impressions are lasting impressions. The doorman, or some other similar first-point of contact employee, is the most important person with regard to guest arrivals. Their warm and sincere smiles, general attentiveness when opening a car or an entrance door, and prompt handling of luggage or requests set the tone for a positive customer experience. Their uniforms and physical gestures convey a first impression of the establishment and their equally important farewell will bring a, hopefully excellent, experience to a close. They also must be aware that the customer's arrival experience begins at the driveway and that guests have plenty of time to observe the doorman's demeanor through their vehicle window while riding up to that entrance or porte-cochere.

Career Tip: Keep in mind that guests may be observing your actions and facial expressions even if you are not aware of their presence. For example, if a guest is sitting in a car, he or she has plenty of time to observe what is going on outside the car windows and who is approaching their vehicle. If the guest is sitting in a lobby, he or she can see beyond the lounge's perimeter. Keep in mind that guests can, and will, be watching your interactions, from a distance and close-up, from every angle.

90 Pushing that Up-selling Edge

Sales pitches that put the customer over the top can be a vicious thing. Up-selling of products is an industry norm, but employees must be trained in the best sales approaches and effectively apply those techniques. Overbearing sales efforts are never a good idea. How many times have you patronized an Italian restaurant and, based on your food and drink selection, knew approximately how much the bill would total only to be surprised that the tab had been increased by another 10-20% due to an eager waiter, pouring from mineral water bottles like crazy. Up-sell with grace and keep your customer's wallet in mind. When customers have a great time and still leave with money in their pockets, they will surely return.

Career Tip: Up-selling is good, but only if the customer does not feel forced into making the purchase. If the customer feels uneasy in his or her response, retreat and let it be. They may buy something else later. If you keep pursuing extra sales, the customers might give in but will most likely leave your establishment with a sour taste in their mouths.

91 Fine Wine, Fine Line

Once I worked in one of Europe's best restaurants. It was so fine that the service staff would sometimes behave better than the guests would. We changed that, by the way, after a nasty review in the newspaper. Then there were these two gentlemen who were there to have dinner. They ordered the big eight-course, $300 menu per person and asked me for wine recommendations.

In true professional spirit, I made the perfect recommendation that best suited their menu sequence. My goal and job were to ensure the best experience that they could have. My wine recommendation was expensive to some but, considering the restaurant, wisely chosen and affordable.

One of the gentlemen thanked me for the recommendation, agreed to it, and said, "But it's only 10 bucks a bottle, isn't it?"

Thinking that he was joking, I played along and said, "Not 10 but 15, Sir." We all laughed, and I proceeded with the order and the suggested wine.

Halfway through the dinner, the guest complimented me on the excellent choice of wine and ordered another. Once again, he said, "Only 15, right?"

With a smile, I said, "Right." Then it came time for the bill.

The same gentleman reviewed his bill and then looked me in the eye. He said, "$100 for a bottle of wine is a lot and, by the way, you said it would only be $15." Any normal member of the staff would have retreated, called the manager, and let him handle the situation, but maybe I was naive or just overly professional. I said, "Yes, Sir, you are correct," changed the bill to $15 per bottle, and presented him with the check.

His male dinner companion was quite disgusted by his friend's behavior and said, "You can't do that!"

Nevertheless, his friend said, "In this restaurant, I can!"

He was right. He paid for the two $300 menus and $30 for the two exquisite bottles of wine. I, on the other hand, lost my hard-earned tips for the next few days, paying the difference out of my own pocket. I was professional enough not only to swallow my financial loss, but also to learn a great lesson about the fine line of not taking a joke over the top between customers and staff.

92 That Empty Hand

One of the first things that I learned in my career in the luxury hospitality industry is never to walk empty-handed. Years later, looking at people in our industry, it seems this idea still needs to be instilled into every employee. All too often waiters walk empty-handed back to the kitchen while the side stations are bursting with dirty and unsightly dishes. All too often, a housekeeper passes a room service tray or trolley in a guest room corridor without pushing it into the nearest lift landing lobby. The examples are too numerous to list. It takes additional training and cross-responsibilities for the concept of never walking empty-handed to become part of an employee's daily routine.

Career Tip: Your productivity, and your company's productivity, can be greatly increased if everyone maximizes their efforts in two ways. Yes, one has to fulfill a task from point A to point B, but think of how much more could be accomplished if people paid attention to performing another task from point B to point A. I have not yet seen this idea included in any training manual.

93 Complaint Principles

While customer complaints are never nice matters to resolve, errors or breakdowns do happen. It is important for managers to protect their employees at all times and personally handle difficult complaints. Customers no longer wish to be taken for granted; they want clear answers and solutions. One big "no-no" is to blame your co-workers and your peers. This is unprofessional and does not solve the matter. The person who receives the complaint should own it. It is difficult and challenging to handling complaints for the first time but doing so will add to your experiences and be of use for the years to come. If your work environment receives the same complaints regularly and repeatedly, it might be time to have a word with your management to discuss the causes of the problems and ways to fix them.

Career Tip: It takes practice to handle different types of customer personalities and complaints. However, in general, if guests complain, they want to see a sincere resolution to their issues right away. Always know the empowerment regulations of your company to determine how far you can go in making decisions without fear of being reprimanded. Also, do not take the customer's complaint light-heartedly or respond in an insincere way. Guests are smart and they do not appreciate or like this type of approach.

94 Customer Fortresses

Why are receptionists, concierges, hostesses, and other counter stationed personnel hiding behind computers screens and desks? I am still unclear on that. Perhaps it gives them that protective, fortress feeling or maybe it shields them from the customer. The bottom line is that there is nothing more unsightly and unfriendly than a customer approaching a front desk with three to five staff members standing behind it, heads down, busily looking at the computer screens. If a customer is lucky, a staff member will see him or her first and respond. In a worst-case scenario, the guest will have to get the staff's attention by greeting them first. Inattentive staff members and barriers to customer service are evidence of a lack of management leadership.

Career Tip: Keep your head high and your eyes focused on your customer at all times. These are some of the most basic, yet important, principles of superior customer service. Even if you work with a computer screen, your eyes are designed with a wider vision range and they are capable of sensing movement, as well as approaching guests. Thus, once your sensor goes off, raise your head and acknowledge your customers.

95 Cost Savings at the Expense of Customers

Cost savings should never affect the guest areas or their experiences. Neither should cost savings hinder the staff's ability to do their jobs. Common practices with regard to guest-related cost savings measures include cutting back on the use of large flower arrangements and removing the pianist from the main lobby. These measures demonstrate a lack of sensitivity with regard to guest appreciation and comfort and, in most cases, these cost-cutting decisions reflect negatively on the business. Customers are no longer immune to sudden changes. If apples have been available on every elevator landing since a guest started staying at your hotel, they still want the apples to be there, even in recessionary economic times. Customers still pay the same price for accommodations and products as they did before the economic downturns so they still want to see the same luxuries.

Career Tip: Cost-saving measures can positively improve a company's bottom line, but this gain in preserving expenses is too often offset by the loss in business due to the unwillingness of many customers to return. Customers will simply question why they are still paying the same price for less thrills and perks. Choose your cost-saving initiatives wisely; make the right calculations before implementing action plans that will cost you customers. If your cost-saving initiative comes top-down from your corporate office 20,000 miles away, be sure to check if these measures are acceptable to your owners and your guests.

96 Get That Unwanted Feeling

Customers can get that unwanted feeling, especially when the breadbasket remains empty, the ice water glass stays unfilled, the bowl of peanuts screams for a refill, or the ashtray (if smoking is still permissible) is overflowing. The cycle of attentive service is not complete until customers have passed through the exit doors of an establishment or property. While there are plenty of annoying scenarios, the ones mentioned above are some of the most common violations that occur in restaurants and bars that affect the customer's opinion of a place, reduce gratuities for the service person, and make a customer's return visit questionable.

Career Tip: Whatever tidbits or special amenities your company decides should to be on guest tables or in guest rooms, ensure that it is always replenished and refreshed. If not, customers will feel cheated and neglected. This does not have to be overdone, but if applied in the right measures, guests will stay happy and will return in the future.

97 Chain Reaction

A customer experience is a chain of events. If one employee happens to break that chain, the whole guest experience could be negatively affected. Guest comment cards are a perfect tool to identify areas where some of the links in this chain may be broken more frequently than others are. Management should pay close attention to this tool and the information that it brings. Once an area is identified, corrective training measures, or process changes, should be put into place.

Career Tip: Guest comment cards can identify areas that need improvement or areas in which you and your team excel. Customers can either condemn or praise your company. Either way, guest comments, whether verbal or written, are a great thing and must be shared with management or operational teams. This important information can then be analyzed and services, as well as products, can be further improved. If customer comments, good or bad, do not reach management, a company is silently sabotaging itself.

98 The Intangible Cost of Loss

Losing customers is a costly expense and the reasons leading to that are often incredibly simple. Customers visit an establishment because of a good experience. They keep going there because the good experiences continue. Then comes the day when this consistency of good experiences is broken. If all the other formulas of this business are right, customers may forgive one off-experience. If they do not, the company will lose that customer forever. In a worst-case scenario, the customer's family, friends, co-workers, and anyone else he or she knows or talks to can potentially become part of the guest's negative reaction to your company. A rule-of-thumb accounting tallies that to 25 disgruntled people. Multiply twenty-five times what a customer would spend, times the number of people they will tell, plus the number of times that they would have returned in a year, and you will get a pretty good understanding of how much money is lost for a year through one dissatisfied customer. The more dissatisfied customers that you have, the greater the negative effect it will have on your company's bottom line and its reputation.

Career Tip: Think about the times that you went somewhere because you liked the place or the product and then one day something happened and you never returned. Was it your hairdresser, your grocer, your dry cleaner, your communications company, or someone else? The same rules apply to your workplace.

99 Process Breakdown

Customer complaints usually arise due to a breakdown within a process. Maybe the staff did not listen properly; maybe an employee did not read the instructions correctly; maybe some of the essential information that was provided was not followed; or maybe a technical glitch caused the problem. In all cases, good staff training could have avoided any of the ensuing issues. If different employees repeat the same mistakes or technical equipment performs inconsistently, it might be helpful to look at the standard operating procedures (SOPs) or processes involved. If discrepancies or faults are detected, gather a group of individuals and launch a problem-solving or process improvement brainstorming session before embarking on work groups and task forces.

Career Tip: Processes are important because they provide a roadmap for both staff and managers. These processes should be frequently reviewed, tested, and updated. Whether the concern involves software or hardware issues, a proactive approach and a good checks and balances system can avoid many unforeseen scenarios.

100 The Knowledgeable Fish Eater

A food and beverage director was once placed in charge of running the operations of a VVIP banquet event with political figures. Before the event, the long-time and experienced chef suggested to the food and beverage manager that he should fully familiarize himself with all the products on the menu for that night. This was because one of the heads of state liked to ask prolonged questions about the menu items.

One such question would be about the fish course. The head of state would ask, "Where did the fish come from?" The answer would be "From Australia." He would ask further, "Where in Australia?" The answer would be "From Tasmania." Again, the head of state would prompt further. "From where in Tasmania?" The answer would be "From Frederick Henry Bay." "How deep was it caught?" the head of state would then ask. The answer would probably be unknown, but if known, could highly impress this guest.

The rationale behind this head of state's questioning was not to embarrass the staff. Rather, he was very familiar with all these regions, their demographics and infrastructures, and he wanted to avoid eating fish from industry-polluted waters due to his health concerns.

The moral of this story is to ask questions all the time. The more that you ask, the more you will know. Chances are that the person you have just asked will also enhance their personal knowledge and be better prepared for the next time you or some other guest comes around seeking information.

Besides, knowledge is fun.

THE HUMAN NATURE

101   A Proper Introduction

Employee orientation for new hires is a common practice among most companies. Unfortunately, this orientation is generalized and applied in the same manner for every rank of employees, who are then dismissed to their assigned departments. The luxury hospitality industry would greatly benefit from employee orientation sessions that are tailored towards specific departments. Let us take a new concierge employee as an example. Once the new employee stands behind the general open desk, he or she will be immediately exposed to customer queries. Customers do not know how long an employee has been working in this job. Unless the employee's nametag indicates that he or she is a trainee, customers are seldom patient if they are in rush for information and that information is not delivered right away. A better approach would be to train the new concierge in a separate area for two to three days after they have concluded the company's orientation program so they are better equipped to interact with customers and respond to customer questions and concerns. If two to three days is not a sufficient amount of time to bring the new concierge up to speed, a longer training time is advised.

Career Tip: A company and its new employees could greatly benefit from a few additional training days or simply a breakdown of the orientation program into modules that specifically apply to different employee groups. This approach will make your newcomers better employees and better prepare them to handle your customers. If newcomers are exposed to possible complaints right at the beginning of their first day of duty, they could become quickly discouraged about their choice of workplace or fail, unexpectedly, in the early stages of their employment. Challenge the human resources department to develop and present two or three different orientation programs, each specific to a group of new hires, instead of mixing everyone, from management to regular staff, in the same two to three day class.

---

102 Qualification Prerequisites

Time is money and a certain amount of speed is required in the workplace. The number of pages a secretary can type in a limited time frame is often part of the interview process. Similarly, finance employees must demonstrate their effectiveness with regard to working through a spreadsheet and a list of numbers. In the hospitality industry, how many times are these types of questions posed to people seeking to be hired as middle or senior managers? Remember that restaurant manager who could not even prepare a simple spreadsheet or that PR person who took two days to write a one-page press release about a simple promotion? There are many more examples of individuals like these in your organization. It is time to either train them to become better in their job or to hire the right person.

Career Tip: Some companies have mastered the art of the interview process and while they may not hit the jackpot every single time, they certainly increase their chances of hiring exceptional employees by carefully testing and selecting new hires. The same principles apply to individuals seeking employment. Make sure that you are qualified for the position and do not overstate your capabilities in your resume or during the interviewing process.

103 Probation Periods

In the busy world of manpower shortage, the all-important one to three month probation rule is more important than ever. Too often, nowadays, newcomers pass the entry tests and multiple interviews, only for it to be discovered, six months down the road, that they are wrong for that job. It is crucial for managers to work with all new individuals for a period of time and to adhere to the periodical reviews and employment evaluations that most companies have. Once that employee passes the probationary period, it will be too late to identify a "bad apple" and your basket of good apples will contain a spoilt one.

Career Tip: While a one to three month probation period is more than adequate, managers need to be more personally involved in training new employees. Managers are lacking in consistency when conducting performance reviews or assessing the capabilities of new hires. Either they let a person that is actually not qualified continue to work or they lose a shining star employee because no one recognized their high potential right from the beginning.

104 Manager Selections

In many cases, unqualified or incompetent management is the downfall of a luxury hotel. Employees will work hard for their properties or company, but if their leaders are not able to do the job on all fronts, a loss in ratings or business volume and dissatisfied staff and customers will ensue. By the time the management or owning company finds out, it is most often too late. Restructuring efforts and rebuilding of what once was is timely and very costly. Thus, it is imperative to use solid interview tools for selecting the right and best possible management candidates.

Career Tip: The luxury hospitality industry is not everyone's cup of tea. While many managers think they are cut out for it, the truth is that they are not and they manage below the property's full potential and standards. Sometimes a manager had a special connection to land the job or perhaps, salary-wise, they were cheaper than the other candidates were. However, very soon the company's initial goodwill or salary-saving decision will backfire.

105 Not Hiring Strong People

Hiring strong employees is easier said than done. Oftentimes, a highly qualified and strong candidate is rejected simply because the interviewer feared that the interviewee might become a potential threat down the road. While he or she may passed the human resources department interview with flying colors, perhaps the final interviewer felt the candidate might be so qualified that they would, eventually, take his or her job down the line. Only wise and professionally secure managers would hire that type of qualified candidate, as they know an employee of such statue and skill would improve the business' performance record and provide the candidate with the opportunity to succeed and continue the legacy of the property or company.

Career Tip: No matter how eager you are to get the job or how qualified you may think you are, be aware of who you are speaking to during your interview. While you may sail through your initial interview with human resources, the interviewers at the next level are potential threats to you. It is a sad, but real, Catch 22. While most companies preach the need for capable and strong people, they are often afraid to hire them if they portray a confident and strong mindset in their interview process.

106 Finding Your Own Replacement

One of my former superiors had a simple principle. The guideline was to find and train your own replacement if you want to be promoted to the next level. Very often, good people become stuck in their positions because they are just too good at what they do and management is hesitant to break that comfort zone and risk disrupting a particularly well run business unit.

Career Tip: Do not be afraid of training your own replacement. Ideally, ensure that this person's skills and talents match your own qualities and that he or she can run the business unit in the same fashion, or even better, than you. No company wants their business unit to underperform suddenly just because you took the safe route of hiring someone that cannot do the job. Doing so will put you back in the position you were seeking to leave, faster than you would imagine.

107 Cultural Diversity

For managers in charge of single or multiple foreign workforces, it is imperative to become informed about the individual culture and customs of their staff. It is not the employees that have to adapt to the manager; it is the manager who has to adapt to his or her staff. There have been too many cases where managers were unprepared and did not know how to deal with employees from foreign cultures. Consequently, they were unable to lead these particular teams effectively, which led to employee dissatisfaction, poor service, and reduced productivity. However, there are those few, selective managers who stay abreast of multicultural issues and concerns and whose staff will climb mountains for them.

Career Tip: One must learn early how to deal with foreign cultures. If you work in a foreign country or with people from a foreign country, adapt and respect their cultures in your best possible manner. If you work in your home country, learn some parts about the culture of the person or persons working for and with you. This will avoid accidental conflicts and make you a better manager.

108 Human Element

I had once started a new senior assignment in a foreign country and, as with all new assignments, I was new to the team and to everyone else. Hence, it took some time to warm up to everyone, especially when I was in charge and from another country.

When I walked the premises, I could feel the eyes of all the staff in the area secretly following me. What is he going to do now? Where is he going next? The staff was not afraid of me, but as a foreigner in their land, they did not quite yet know how to approach me. The managers were fine, but I am talking about everyone else, from young receptionists to service staff in the restaurants.

Then, the day came when, after a six-month absence due to giving birth, my wife returned from overseas with our newborn baby daughter. The next day, I went to the lobby and, again, all eyes were on me. A few moments later, the elevator doors opened, my wife and baby daughter came towards me, and my wife handed me our cute little baby. I grabbed her, held her close to my chest, and kissed her on the cheeks and forehead. In turn, she grabbed my glasses, pulled my nose, and drooled all over my suit. In that very same moment, every single eye and face that had me under observation just moments before changed. Their eyes got bigger and their respectful and serious facial expressions turned into big warm smiles. You could feel that the burden had lifted from their chests once they saw that I was just a loving father and human after all. From that day onwards, eyes still followed me around, but when met, the staff sent warm, sincere, and trusting smiles my way.

109 Who Works for Whom

Employees do not work for you; they work for the company and you work with them. A fundamental misperception of many managers is that the employee becomes their property once they have entered the doors of their new workplace. The only ownership a manager can take with regard to these individuals is to attend to their well-being and nurture them professionally during their time with the company. Managers should do their utmost to mentor their employees in order to foster the talents of as many hospitality professionals as possible. The more employees who graduate from this experience, the better the hospitality industry will become in the future.

Career Tip: Taking full ownership of one's job, department, or property is the right thing to do. However, do not step over the fine line and personalize things with regard to your staff. Instead, treasure these individuals and see them as partners of all ages. They are part of a team that will help you succeed.

110 Traditional Training Methods

In many companies, a review of general training procedures for operational and administrative staff is long overdue. Unfortunately, too many organizations are still fixated on the traditional methods of training. In today's world of fast-paced technology, the younger generation is no longer interested in the long-winded and slow training process. Like any of us, they want information; they want it now; and they want it packaged as simply and as attractively as possible with the instant ability to apply what they learn. This could be easily achieved through the re-education of training managers who thereafter can produce high-tech video and audio presentations.

Career Tip: New ventures and independent properties often draw from whatever manuals and standards their first team brought with them and adopt them accordingly. The issues are primarily related to time constraints and are caused by failed planning in the early stages of a project. To make a business unique and stand out over time, new companies should make it a practice to engage teams to develop and write training plans as soon as the vision for a new project is born. Based on that initial vision and on the specific project-related environment and demographics, training manuals should be crafted with precision to suit the particular needs of this project.

111 Demographic Personalities

Demographic personalities play an important role in the success of any luxury hospitality company. People who live near oceans generally have a more open mindset, with a wider horizon, than those who live in enclosed mountain regions. People from the south are generally more passionate and warmer than those who live in the north. An understanding of demographic personalities can help you better understand the needs of your co-workers and your guests and will enable you to apply the appropriate attributes needed to foster good customer and staff relationships. There are also plenty of reference books available for you to study demographic personalities in more depth. Ultimately, the more that you know about your co-workers and customers, the more successful you, and your business, will be.

Career Tip: Knowing about your co-workers' cultural strengths and weaknesses or customers' demographics, likes, dislikes, habits, and preferences can help you to foster stronger relationships and apply the right methods for success. It is an employee's responsibility, in the front of the house and in the back of the house, to find out as much of this information as possible.

112 Company Basics

It is essential for every employee to learn, understand, and practice company basics. In most cases, these basics are always there, but if you do not know them by heart and do not practice them whole-heartedly every day, you stand a chance of depriving yourself of the opportunity to be successful and to be happy. Companies do not write these basic rules for no good reason. They are simplified versions of comprehensive rules to make your life easier and help you perform better. Companies that do not have a set of basic rules should seriously develop and implement some.

Career Tip: In general, company basics, credos, and mission statements will tell you a great deal about the company in which you are about to work. These little extracts and sentences are often highly compressed to provide you with a powerful roadmap of what to do and how things should be done within the work environment.

113 Speed of Learning

Young people can learn the features of their new hand-held phone or video game in an instant, but how long does it take a manager to instill some operational techniques in a young person's mind? In order to get the younger generation to adopt new practices and methods, it is important to use faster training approaches that tap into their ability to learn quickly. Doing so will help a manger properly and effectively train this new generation of workers.

Career Tip: Training a younger generation of workers, who are fast learners, is a tough issue that companies face today. Smart managers will try to find that special employee in their company who can get through to these young employees of today.

114 Conflicts

Every employee will be involved in a conflict with a co-worker or peer at some point in his or her career. If the concern or issue at the center of this conflict is not worth pursing, step back and let the other person have their way. If you are absolutely confident that you are correct, stand your ground. An exception to this, of course, is if the conflict is between you and your supervisor and he or she is confident that he or she is right. In such cases, you should still raise your concerns and present the facts, but in the end, your superior will have the final say. If the superior happens to be right in the end, watch and learn; if he or she was wrong, do not rub it in spitefully. Instead, learn from the experience and remember what not to do.

Career Tip: People have different personalities and different beliefs. Think twice before making a hardheaded comment or decision and be sure that you are absolutely right before blaring out statements that are not reversible.

115 Working with Bad Apples

Stay away from people who may affect your performance and hinder your ability to fulfill your duties with the company. If a co-worker is grumpy or gets off to a bad start one day, try to cheer them up. If several attempts fail, move on and concentrate on the job and the tasks ahead. In the worst case scenario, if the other person disrupts your performance, have the courage to alert the manager. It is the manager's job to deal with that co-worker and try to help resolve the issue.

Career Tip: Unhappy people are like quicksand and, thus, should be approached with caution. They can affect your life and work performance in many ways, but most often in a negative manner rather than a positive one. Unhappy people can be found among senior ranks or junior ranks so keep your eyes open at all times.

116 Telephone Operators/PBX

Telephone operators are often neglected and staff turnover in that department is very high. Not only does this lead to frequently inexperienced staff, but also to customer dissatisfaction, as newcomers just cannot be trained and familiarized fast enough. An operator, or PBX, department, as it is sometimes called, is often stuck in the far corners of a building, in a workplace that lacks windows and natural light and air. Management and other executives in charge of this department should make regular visits, throughout the day and night, to keep in close contact with these staff members and ensure that this team receives the special recognition it deserves and is not forgotten by the company

Career Tip: The telephone operator/PBX department is the voice of any company. Even if most of a company's employees will never personally hear these voices, the customers certainly will and they will judge your company image by the tone of the first words that they hear from these operators. Working in an environment like this could be fun if management attempts to create a pleasant experience for these employees. Ultimately, company attention will have a positive effect on the telephone operators/PBX employees working in this office.

117 That Heart of the House

Back of the house facilities are as important as front of the house facilities. The employees' restroom and changing facilities should be friendly, clean, and sanitized. Furthermore, the lift landings, walls, and corridor floors should be free of damage, and storerooms, as well as walk in refrigerators, should be kept insanely clean. Companies that do not adhere to strict guidelines for their back of the house facilities are prone to cases of food poisoning and higher incidences of employee accidents.

Career Tip: Back of house facilities will always fall apart if management does not frequently visit and attend to these areas. It is imperative to stay on top of things in this area before health departments or uncalled-for accidents force you to do so.

118 Generational Expectation Bar

When dealing with staff members who are 10 to 20 years younger, we often catch ourselves setting the expectation bar really high. The rationale for this runs along the lines of "Well, they did it to me, so I have the right of doing it to them." While you might be justified in holding this perception, if you apply it to young employees, very often they will start doubting their capabilities and their choice of a career in the luxury hospitality industry. Two rules should be applied. One is to place yourself in the shoes of this individual and travel mentally back in time to when you were the same age. Where you personally ready to handle this task at that age? The other rule is to ensure that you are helping the individual complete the assigned task successfully and gain knowledge, as well as confidence, from it.

Career Tip: As soon as young employees start in your company, a parental approach should be adopted. If you care for these young individuals as if they were part of your family, your approach will automatically be more that of a mentor than an autocrat.

119 Proper Delegation of Ideas

Delegating your personal ideas can often be tricky and may lead to disappointment. It is important that you know each person's capabilities and skills before you assign ideas to others. If you delegate solely based on rank and title, you may be in for a surprise and an outcome that is far from your original expectations. Doing it yourself, or with some team members, is always a good idea and sets the proper height for the expectation bar. Thereafter, you can let your team members do it themselves. In this way, you will avoid distress and only have to invest a small amount of time to make corrections and move forward.

Career Tip: Get to know the special capabilities of your staff and then train those who need assistance before you begin delegating. Be sure to also ensure that your ideas are precisely formulated, that co-workers know what your expectations are, and that they understand they can turn to you for questions if need be. Every person has their own mindset and ways of interpreting ideas unless they are working with clearly defined technical ideas that have specific and detailed guidelines.

120 "Won't Work" - Creativity Killers

The expressions, "That won't work" and "We can't do that" are creativity killers. Using these phrases with your staff only leads to a demoralizing work environment and a "can't do" attitude. To solicit suggestions from your staff or team members and fuel their passions support all their creative ideas. Remember, every idea is a good idea. Only time will tell which ideas will make it into the final selection and which ideas will not.

Career Tip: Foster and encourage staff participation as much as possible. If your team feels that you are seriously committed to open mindedness, they will soon submit ideas on their own. The result will be continued improvement and growth within your department or company.

121 The Ease of Brainstorming

Brainstorming sessions can be very successful if a) the audience is highly motivated; b) the topic is very interesting; and c) the team is on a mission. If these conditions are not possible and you still wish to gather different ideas, try a different approach. Hand out a stack of Post-It Notes to all the people at the table or in the room. Select the topic and ask them to write down each idea and stick the note onto a white board. There is no need for people to sign their names. This will take the pressure off the person and, in turn, will encourage them to make suggestions freely without being judged. A group of 25 to 30 people will easily be able to generate 80 to 120 ideas in less than 10 minutes. Be sure that you tabulate each idea/submission on a summary sheet and share these at your next meeting, as this will foster a continued will to participate.

Career Tip: The Post-It Notes session is an easy approach and can bring some very good results as long as you keep the session genuine. For some reason, this method takes the pressure off people and lets them participate in a more relaxed manner.

122 Staff Restaurant

In some organizations, the staff canteen is often the last place on Earth anyone wants to be unless management eats there as well or the company really makes an effort to take good care of its employees. Employee meals are a big cost item on an organization's expense sheets. While some companies are proud of what they offer their employees, others pay little attention to this company perk. For any hotel, the staff canteen should be the most important restaurant in the organization. This is the sanctuary where the staff recharges, socializes with each other, rests their minds, and prepares for that next shift to face their customers. If a company contracts the staff canteen out to another organization, it is important to add extra touches to the menu periodically during special company occasions and holidays. Management should also be sure to make it a habit to visit frequently, check on the well-being of their staff, and investigate how the menu looks that day.

Career Tip: A staff canteen is the nerve center of your operation. If you keep this area in great shape and ensure that your staff is satisfied with what it has to offer, your employees will naturally be happier. Make frequent checks on the food preparation and dish-out areas. Ensure that food selection choices, as well as food preparation, is up to par. If you do not feel appreciation coming your way from your employees, be sure to have a word with the people responsible for this area.

123 Paying Attention to the A-Teams

The easiest ways to motivate your staff is by sharing knowledge with them, appraising them, positively challenging them, and trusting them. These four little points will create a powerful concoction for building a strong dream team. Every organization has one or more superstar teams and, if you look closely, in 9 out of 10 cases, it is the management person or leader that is responsible for that team's success. Unfortunately, dysfunctional teams get the most attention from upper management while the superstar teams are very quickly taken for granted. If you are from upper management and are responsible for a superstar team within your division, make sure to periodically visit them and recognize the contributions of the team and its leader.

Career Tip: Take advantage of your superstar managers, either by promoting them to help with more areas or by selectively assigning them occasional involvement in areas that need training or other assistance. Never take these individuals for granted; they work hard to bring you and your company the results you desire.

124 The Brown-Nose

Very few people appreciate a brown-noser, those employees who will, seemingly, say or do anything to get in the good graces of their supervisors. It is important to note that being a brown-noser is not a positive career attribute. Sometimes brown-nosers are simply people who crave attention. If you fall victim to them, good luck. The actions of a brown-noser does little else than unnecessarily consume your energy and it does not guarantee success.

Career Tip: Be aware that most people seriously dislike the tactics employed by brown-nosers. Being a brown-noser can affect your ability to rise within your company. It could have an adverse effect on your managers, as well as on your peers and the co-workers that work with you. Therefore, always keep a clean performance sheet and reroute your energies to where they are need most.

125 American Idiom in Japanese

A long time ago, on a beautiful Japanese afternoon, there seemed to be trouble in paradise. The location was one of Japan's first international hotels and it was boosted by business.

One of their busy venues was the lobby lounge, a place where 200-250 Japanese ladies would gather every afternoon to enjoy western cakes and other sweet temptations. Although there was usually a predictable business pattern, that day seemed to be different. For some reason, the new manager managed to make the guest in the lounge uncomfortable. Their discomfort not only resulted in the breakdown of operational processes, but the clientele, who were normally patient, were beginning to become irritated with the long waiting lines at the entrance. Unknowingly, and with little preparation, I walked right into the middle of it.

While the manager did what he could and tried his best, a simple call for help would have been sufficient. The problem was that although the first wave of guests had enjoyed the plentiful cakes and savories, the kitchen could no longer keep up with replenishment, resulting in delays when serving guests, as well as a reduction in the known turnover cycle for tables. The result was the formation of a queue at the entrance.

It took about one minute to walk the floor and judge the state of every table, another minute to assess the situation in the kitchen and pastry department, and another to gauge the situation at the entrance. Thereafter, quick thinking and a good portion of judgment and decision-making were in order. The first decision was to summon the big guys from the kitchen and instruct them to ensure that the cake production needs and speed were secured immediately. Then it was time to calm the manager and place him in charge of a single task: to ensure that the buffet was five-star in presentation and stayed replenished until the end. Last but not least, the decision to take charge of managing the venue personally was a wise one.

With 80 ladies in the queue and an entrance team that was stressed beyond belief, I walked up to them … actually, before I continue, it must be said that I was the only non-Japanese speaker and the only foreigner visible to my team and to the ladies at that time. I looked at the guests in line and my staff and said, "ASAMESHI-MAE," which pretty much equates to the idiom "piece of cake," meaning "that's easy!" I instantly received a relieved look from my staff and guests. About 15 minutes later, everything was back under control and everyone enjoyed delicious cakes happily ever after.

IN OPERATIONS

126 Safety Comes First

Safety is one of the most, if not the most, important aspect of a work environment in this industry. Never take safety light-heartedly and always adhere to the rules and regulations of the company's standard operating manuals or what you have been taught. The well-being of employees is at stake, as is the well-being of the many guests staying in or visiting the facilities. There are so many things to consider and take note of — from slippery pool areas to slippery back of the house kitchen floors, from clogged staircase exits to overcapacities in venues, from the chef that taught you how to hold a knife correctly to the bellman that showed you how to avoid a back injury when carrying luggage. The rules and regulations, manuals, or warnings of what not to do, in most cases, have been written after something has already happened and someone has gotten hurt. Be careful. Be safe. Do not get hurt or cause someone else to get hurt.

Career Tip: Every company has some sort of safety guidelines that describe scenarios of how to avoid accidents in the workplace or how to react in an emergency. Make it a habit to read those manuals when you first become an employee and practice safety every day. Do not be afraid to point out areas of concern to others.

127 That Clean Carpet

Clean hotel guest room carpets are a sign of a well-maintained facility and are essential to the successful retention of female travellers. Wonder why? Many women wear high heels and look forward to slipping out of those painful shoes after they return to their hotel room. Not everyone likes those free 20-cent hotel slippers and if a woman cannot walk barefoot on a carpet due to unsightly stains and spots, she may opt quickly to go to another hotel — the one that your company calls a competitor, where the carpets are soft, pristine, and worthy of being walked upon barefoot.

Career Tip: From supervisory staff to senior management, routine inspections to insure a well-maintained facility are a must. The guest room is the main product for hotels and resorts and if carpets, among other things, are repulsive, clients will not return or may cut short their stay. Carpet replacement should be a standard item listed on the annual capital expenditure list.

128 Some Old Rules Still Apply

Old rules still apply. A dirty public toilet and a dirty kitchen scream: "Don't go there." A torn or stained hotel bedroom sheet or fingerprints on the mini-bar glass say: "Don't use this." A hair in the shower or sink says: "This is not properly clean." The list is very long. Every employee knows what to do; however, after a while, most people do not do the things they know they should do. Therefore, it is important to continuously conduct spot-checks and inspections, provide re-training for existing staff whenever necessary, and ensure that everyone is well aware of the company's high standards of cleanliness and excellence.

Career Tip: Guests are very quickly appalled if they spot that little leftover residue. It is unhygienic and customers will very quickly hold that against you and your company. No matter how high or low the price paid for a room or facility, when it comes to hygiene, a customer has a clear set of expectations that must be met.

129 Z-Vision

A manager is in charge of everything within the business unit. This also includes many items and areas to which he or she sometimes cannot relate. Ceilings, walls and floors, and anything within that 3-dimensional room are part of a manager's job. Very often managers do not see it that way; instead, they point their fingers at the department that handles these areas and feel that the case is closed after a short phone call to that respective supervisor in charge. This is not only a fundamental mistake that managers often make, but it also shows a great lack of caring for one's facility. The point-of-finger rule applies in these cases. One finger points to that department, but three fingers still point back at you, the manager. Never forget that.

Career Tip: Get used to the Z-vision when walking your premises. A Z-vision is looking at the ceiling, down the walls, and everything in sight before you reach the floor. This way you will detect nearly all the little flaws that come to view. If you make this a habit, it will be become natural and even that tiny cobweb in the corner of a ceiling, or a nearly invisible stain on the marble floor, will not escape your eyes.

130 Consistency

In another part of the world, there was a famous luxury hotel that had a signature drink, which sold up to 2,000+ portions on a busy day. After a while, the company decided to use machines for the production of this drink in their bars. The simple reason for this was that human preparation could no longer guarantee a consistent product every time, all the time.

So, fresh juices were mixed and poured into containers every morning and then locked to avoid tampering. Then, another locked container containing the alcoholic concoction was placed next to it. Now, all the bartender had to do was to place ice into the glass, push the button, and add a garnish. The result was a perfect signature drink that tasted the same at 10 AM on one day as it did at 10 PM on another.

While some people may object to this procedure, let me tell you what happened afterwards. A few years later, the company decided to convert some of their grounds to additional bars. This was no big deal, but the problem was that there was no space to install the mixing machine for the signature drink. Therefore, the management had to fall back on the good old human production of mixing it from scratch and by hand. The drink was served so many times a day that the color became like a blueprint embedded in my head.

One day, as I walked the premises, I happened to look at one of the new outdoor bars from a distance. My best guess is that it stood about 80 feet away from where I was standing. For some reason, I stopped and observed two guests patronizing the bar counter and a bartender preparing the famous signature drink. As he was about to place the two signature drinks on the counter in front of the guests, I noticed that the color of the drink was much lighter than it should have been. This was a clear sign of a concoction that had been poured over watered-down cubes of ice.

Against my nature and with much discomfort, I whistled loudly into the open. While the guests did not really know where the whistling was coming from, the bartender suddenly froze, turned around, and looked at me. After all, I was the only person standing with a suit in the tropical distance. He knew instantly. He quickly removed the two signature drinks from the counter, before the guests had a chance to sip them, and replaced them with two perfect ones.

Dedicated managers cannot be everywhere all the time, but it is so important to instill quality into the mindset of employees of all ages.

131 No Longer Valid

Over the years, it has become imperative to train Plans B and C in addition to A. Take a look at this example of a simple restaurant service procedure. All items must be served from the right and cleared from the right. While this general rule was easy to apply in the spacious dining rooms of the past, in today's cramped and maximized establishments, this rule is often no longer valid or even possible at times. Instead, teach wait staff to serve from the side. This method inconveniences the guest the least and avoids the possibility of the service personnel being stuck in an awkward position.

Career Tip: Basic training procedures should vary from environment to environment and be adapted to staff and guests alike. Review your company's basic training manual and take the time to rewrite the sections that are in need of revision to suit your particular operational set up.

132 Knowing One's Forte

Very often, you will find executive chefs in charge of multiple restaurants with cuisines ranging from Continental to Japanese and Mexican to Chinese. In most cases, these senior managers, or culinary directors, like to eat the food prepared at their restaurants, but they can barely manage the basics required of the individual cuisines. Even highly accomplished executive chefs should invest time and learn about the areas, products, and preparations for which they are responsible. It will not only boost their personal egos and knowledge levels, it will be a great motivation for their staff. Of course, there are those very few executive chefs who are experts in all cuisines and who are highly respected.

Career Tip: Have you ever seen a director of rooms who actually cannot jump-in behind the reception desk at any given time to assist with heavy check-in volumes because he does not know the functionality of the operating system or a culinary director who never visits specialty kitchens due to the complexity of certain product specifications and preparations? Managers who do not try to understand the basic procedures in their own work areas will be unable to support and teach their staff. Moreover, if managers can be seen avoiding these areas, due to fear of involvement the operation of these areas will be thrown out of balance.

133 A Business with No Soul

Floor managers, or lobby managers, are the important guards of the hospitality industry. Guests come to hotels, restaurants, and bars to be pampered and to see and meet the guys in charge. Of course, there will always be plenty of regular staff around but, as with any business, every place needs a soul. In most cases, the floor manager or one of the top executives is selected to fulfill that function. Brush up on your office productivity, reset your priorities, and get out there to greet your guests at different times of the day.

Career Tip: Too often investors have built dream buildings, which sometimes can cost hundreds of millions of dollars, but they fail to engage management that is dedicated to face-to-face time with their guests. No matter how fancy or expensive a place is, it will quickly become a hollow statement if its leaders do not interact with the guests. In the industry, people refer to those grand or luxury hotels as a place without a soul, meaning that there is no one in charge who manages the place by, and with, heart.

134 Bottlenecks

Bottlenecks are common scenarios in operations that are unable to plan and prepare in advance. Too often, the scheduling and planning of operational rosters is delegated down the line to the supervisory newcomer who is unable to read the demand curves accurately. This results in customers who start to form a line and/or back of the house operations that are literally backed up. People will begin to suffer; stress levels will rise to their limits; and, in the end, no one, including customers and the staff, will leave with a positive experience that day. Managers must commit themselves to handling the planning of peak times until they find the right person to whom they can delegate this task.

Career Tip: Bottlenecks are a form of too much volume coming your way too quickly. Once a bottleneck is formed, you, your staff, and your customers face an uphill battle. If the business you work in is popular, prepare accordingly for the customer volumes associated with that level of success. Appropriate planning and proactive management can avoid bottleneck scenarios, which can distress customers and staff alike.

135 Peak Time Management

Operational peak times are known in every business unit of an organization. Point of sale (POS) software can easily churn out reports for outlets; Opera software can do the same for room-related departments; and BOH systems can do it for every other area. These reports are readily available but are rarely requested. If managers would ask for them, they could effectively schedule their staff rosters based on the available information. This, in turn, can limit customer satisfaction concerns, help you avoid understaffed situations, and eliminate the unnecessary stress that is placed on a handful of dedicated employees.

Career Tip: Peak time management information is almost always available. Simply ask for it, review it, and do something with it. If you do not, skip the preceding paragraph and prepare for lower customer satisfaction ratings.

136 Body and Mind Chess

Sometimes, business is like a game of chess. If you do not play your strategies and figures right, you may lose — sometimes right away, sometimes a little later. In business particularly, the correct distribution of bodies in a work area, and its associated strategy, can be the deciding factor between success and failure. Just because that old, pre-existing, manning guide indicates the numbers of bodies required to staff a particular area adequately, does not mean that the figures are still correct. Business dynamics or market trends may have changed since then. If the business has slowed and stays that way, adjust the manning downwards and shift the bodies into other areas of need. If the business has dramatically increased — I mean number of guests, and not just necessarily revenue, add bodies to handle the demand in an appropriate manner.

Career Tip: Establish a sensory heat scan for your business. The more guests you have and the greater the workload you experience can be represented as heat (the color red). Empty areas or lesser workloads can be represented as cold (the color blue). If these areas require human labor to balance the heat, add more staff; if the areas require more tools, add more software and machines that can handle the load.

137 Wrongly Placed Efforts

If sales managers or salespersons are worried that their operational departments cannot live up to the promises they have made to their customers, they very often dedicate their personal time in that operation to safeguard their customers. While it might help and the customers might leave happy, managers will lose valuable time that could have been used to foster new clients, complete an important trend chart or market study, or reply to the numerous enquiries that they receive in a timely manner. In this Catch 22, both issues will affect that salesperson's performance as well as the overall performance of the company. Furthermore, good sales staff will often leave for other companies in their search of greener pastures or more reliable operational teams.

Career Tip: Operational teams must be able to deliver on customer promises made by the company's sales force. The salesperson is a single individual who sells the customer experience in its entirety, but this experience can only be executed by various operational teams. A common, and very immature, mistake among operational teams is to see the salesperson as the person from the other side. Ensure that frequent meetings take place between sales and operational teams. These meetings will assist in breaking down that invisible barrier and give the people a chance to get to know about each other. Most importantly, it will give them an opportunity to hear about and better understand the role and contributions of the sales force and how the company's products are being promoted.

138 SOP Managers

Managers, and more experienced staff that are hiding behind SOPs, are apprehensive to change and often dilute motivated newcomers who try to improve things with their new ideas. A new employee will come to work with an open mind and see things differently. A good approach for managers and experienced staff is to momentarily step back from their powerful positions to hear out these employees. In many cases, the new idea makes sense, is up-to-date with current customer trends, and does not require that much effort to implement. While SOPs are, of course, necessary, they should be reviewed frequently in the luxury hospitality industry. Hospitality is not a manufacturing business that lives by stringent guidelines. Instead, the hospitality industry deals with human beings, whose behaviors change more rapidly than an SOP can be updated. For example, the idea to include social networking website links on the company's website came from a young, newly hired employee, not from a veteran senior manager in charge of that department. Many changes are necessary in this industry, but it takes people with foresight, sensible intuition, and determination for those changes to happen.

Career Tip: SOPs that directly relate to customer service are especially important and should be reviewed more often than others. Experienced managers should invest more time and interact with new employees, or a company's human resources department should implement brainstorming sessions to tap into the minds of creative individuals right from the beginning. The new generation of employees is well experienced in current trends and their generation's behaviors are similar to those of your new clientele. Review your manuals and check to see how many new SOPs have been written to address information technology and other communication gadgets, which your clientele travels with these days. Or spend a weekend in your banquet department, where hundreds of young people attended a prom or a graduation party. Young people are your guests of tomorrow, and they are growing up fast. Do not leave them out of your business plans.

139 Chocolate on the Pillow

Guests appreciate the little amenities, such as chocolate on the pillow before going to bed. It is amazing that, after all these decades, things have not changed that much. It all comes down to amenity expenses. If your organization cannot afford to place chocolates on the pillows of guests, or if it is time to introduce a different amenity, a bit of creativity is required on the part of the director of rooms or an associated manager to address this issue.

Career Tip: Turndowns and many other amenities are very infrequently changed or reinvented. While they are part of those little, important customer service touches a company has to offer, there is no harm in asking think-tank groups to come up with something new occasionally.

140 Come Out from Wherever You Are

Today, good managers are people who do not ask a guest for his or her name and personal details after their twentieth visit. Instead, they have learned to take advantage of systems and customer history information. They come out of their offices or away from their desks to greet guests by name. Face-to-face interaction is still the most valuable form of customer recognition. Some managers are reluctant to leave their safe and comfortable office environment and so they leave customer interactions to their "little soldiers," the employees at the registration counter or in the room. These managers think that their personal presence is only required if something goes really wrong or if a customer requests to speak to them to compliment them on their staff's exceptional service.

Career Tip: A common industry problem occurs when managers very quickly occupy themselves with administrative work, or other non-operational work, during peak times. They misperceive that everything is in motion now and they are free to attend to other things. This attitude often causes the problems in the first place. This is because managers are supposed to anticipate things in advance and ensure that issues are avoided before they can occur. Managers must be available and on the floor when customers are present. They should find other, more appropriate times, to complete their administrative and non-operational duties.

141 Habits and Routines

Guests have habits and routines and they do not appreciate it when these are disrupted. Whether a customer travels a lot or seeks tranquility, he or she prefers that their things remain untouched. In a hotel room, for example, a housekeeper should put things back where they found them. Little gestures go a long way. If a shampoo bottle is empty, it is nice to have a fresh one when the guest returns. If a guest's laptop is set on the table in a particular way, putting it in the same position, regardless of company standards, goes a long way to building customer satisfaction.

Career Tip: Pay attention to the little details when entering a guest's room. If the guest stays with you for more than one day, this will give you a chance to observe and be more detailed in your approach. If the guest is a repeat customer, share this information with your manager or, if available, place it into the guest history software program. Customers who are the least disrupted by the little things and who feel recognized and greeted every time they return can become great ambassadors for your company.

142 Guest Room Phobia

Once a guest checks into a hotel room, he or she might become irritated by the clutter of different promotional items, hotel announcements, and welcome letters that he or she finds on the guest room desk when trying to free up some space in that area. This is a typical case of how no one associated with managing the guest's room environment — from the director of rooms and the director of food and beverages, to the director of sales and marketing — gave proper instructions on how to make this environment more guest-friendly. Frequent management changes can also have the same affect. Guests might find seven different shades of brown among the stationary folders, pads, mini bar sleeves, and remote control covers after a couple of years because nobody on staff paid attention to the replacement guidelines or added a little extra personal touch to how these items were arranged for the guest's use.

Career Tip: If you inherit a style, you must own it. If you do not like it for any reason, plan to change the entire list of items. If you only change one thing, for example, because of budget restraints, you do more harm to the area than good. Spend some time in the guest rooms to place yourself in the shoes of your travelling guests and then determine how well the room set up works.

143 Staff Status Beliefs

The ultimate chef is the person who prepares the order exactly the way the customers asked it to be prepared and puts his or her personal beliefs aside. Guests have habits and they know how they like their food and beverages to be prepared. Not everyone is a connoisseur who eagerly entrusts their dining experience to the vision of the chef. Some people just hate to break with their habits. Thus, a steak well-done means well-done, and extra salt means extra salt. The same applies to other guest requests in bars, guest rooms, and recreational facilities.

Career Tip: Never try to impose your status as a hotel or restaurant upon your guests. You may have a great name and reputation, but do not take your customers for granted. Just because the culinary maestro feels it is perfect, which it may be, the customer should be able to enjoy his meal the way he wants it. If a customer wants more salt or pepper on his steak, take care of it. If a customer wants his expensive red wine bottle at a certain temperature, do not try to educate him to the contrary. Simply satisfy the customer's requests.

144 Mega Assumptions

If you are assigned the task of planning and executing a mega function this year, here are some helpful pointers. Spend as much time as you can on attending to all the details of executing this plan. Do not leave things to chance and de not assume anything. Assumptions can very often lead to negative surprises, especially as the day of the event draws near. Always be consistent in your follow-ups on all delegated matters. As soon as possible, try to imagine the entire event, from beginning to the end, in your mind. Play out A, B, and C scenarios and try to solve any possible glitches prior to the event date. With all that pre-planning and mental rehearsing, you will be on your way to a successfully executed event.

Career Tip: Big events mean big responsibilities. It also means a big audience and big profits if you plan and execute it right. Therefore, never fall prey to assumption. While, of course, you have to trust your co-workers, and everyone else involved in the project, be sure to double- and triple-check every detail, as often as you can— whether this is your first event or your 100th event, whether this is your first time working with this team or your 20th time. Follow these guidelines and, from here on out, future events will be a piece of cake.

145 Restaurant Managers

Restaurant managers come in a variety of personalities, work habits, and temperaments. Their performances are varied as well. One thing is certain, however, they are supposed to manage; they are not to appease their hostesses, clear trays, hide behind the kitchen food-pass, or drink coffee in the office during operational hours. Managers must manage, pure and simple. Some simple rules for effective management include: a) welcome all guests personally and log their arrival time in your mind; b) once the first batch of reservations is seated, make rounds and check all tables; c) if any irregularities are obvious (such as the guests, who were seated 10 minutes ago, still do not have water or bread at the table), stop, discern the cause, and utilize your management skills to remedy the situation as soon as possible; and d) repeat a, b, and c until all reservations are in and then spend the rest of the meal period on the floor with your guests and staff until the shift is finished. Thereafter, praise your staff for a job well done, get a cup of coffee, and finish that spreadsheet in your office.

Career Tip: If you happen to be a restaurant manager who is reading this book right now, remember one thing: you are the soul and mind of your company's operation. The more that you care about your customers and staff, the more you will be successful and respected. It is understood that A, B, C, and D seem highly simple, but if you do not practiced these steps daily, and with determination, your restaurant will fail in the long run.

146 Handling of a Mega Event

One day, my then general manager summoned me into the office. The general manager said that we had the opportunity to host a reception for 1,200 and 1,500 guests, respectively. Before I continue, it must be mentioned that this particular hotel had previously never hosted any events larger than 600 guests. I instantly said two things. First, I said that I had no problem with this. Second, I said that it must be at a price that would do justice to our premises and efforts. The general manager looked me in the eye and smiled; after all, I was the one in charge of a massive operation that had many, many restaurants and I was the one who had to handle it all with my teams.

The next step was to get the organizer of the company that wanted to host these two events, the operational team leaders, and myself together. Everything, including a lucrative price, was agreed upon and the deal was signed. Luckily, we had three-quarters of a year to prepare.

The menu planning was already off to an unanticipated start. I told my chef that I needed two menus, one for each night for the 1,200 and 1,500 guests, respectively. In turn, he sent me the usual, pre-planned banquet menus on file. Big mistake! I made a pledge of superior choice and quality in line with the hotel's reputation, and while the pre-planned menus were excellent for regular events, this one needed extra touches and detailed preparation.

Therefore, I called the chef to my office at 8 PM that night and welcomed him with a pile of empty paper. Armed with a pen, I made it very clear that this event needed extra special attention and that we were now going to write the menu together. As stated earlier, we had many, many restaurants with pretty much everything that the culinary world had to offer, and I was adamant that not one, but all of the kitchens should participate. So we began. We spent the next seven hours (until 3 AM) finishing our menu draft. It was wonderful. We brainstormed, discussed, argued, and agreed. In the end, the menu that came out of it was fantastic and even made my mouth water just by reading it. I kept a copy and gave the original to him for his secretary to type. She nearly fainted when she saw the many pages the next day. Planning and preparations had started!

There were so many things to plan that it made my adrenaline levels rise each day. It was overwhelming! However, for some reason, it was also no big deal. We planned and rehearsed for everything: Plan A, Plan B, and so forth. I found myself preaching one thing all the time; it is possible, no matter how hard or difficult the resistance.

On the actual day itself, I was everywhere from early in the morning onwards, checking, re-checking, and checking everything again. Once the guests arrived, the teams kicked into execution mode, and what a sight it was! There were 200 chefs and God knows how many waiters all ready to deliver on our promise. And it turned out to be a most magical evening for all our guests. The high adrenaline levels retreated after the last guest left and we all knew that 48 hours later, we had the same thing to do again, but this time with even more guests.

On the day of the second event, I faced a serious problem. I began inspecting everything as usual starting at 5 AM in the morning, but this time it was different. While I tried to find areas where advice for improvements was appropriate, I instead found myself having cafe lattes every two hours because there was nothing to complain about or to correct. That continued throughout the day and throughout the function. The beautiful thing was that everyone who initially said that it was impossible learned from the first function. This means that people do learn that impossible is only a border that needs to be breached. Hence, the execution of the second event was even better than that of the first.

Bottom line and result? I was so proud of the teams and deeply touched that from then onwards, nothing was impossible. Moreover, for those people within our teams, no matter where and what they are doing now, nothing continues to be impossible for them today.

147 Old World Struggles

Old world struggles are common between teams. Has a chef ever given you a plate that was glowing hot and burned your fingers? Have you ever held back on all your customer orders with the intention of slamming the kitchen with intense stress levels or delayed responding to a call for assistance from your peers and co-workers? These old world struggles happen all the time. The best way to avoid this negative behavior is by doing your best to get along with people and never be on the wrong side of an issue. Petty actions do not pay off, nor do they go a long way in building trust and respect among your peers. Petty acts do not go down so well with customers or with managers, either.

Career Tip: Sadly, old world struggles still happen in too many places when people take advantage of their areas or positions. Do not fall into this trap. Remember that knowledge is king and so is leading by example.

148 Taken for Granted but Really Important

Hotel engineers or technicians have some of the most thankless jobs in this industry. While they are actually hired to maintain the equipment and facilities of a hotel or asset, they quickly become trouble-shooters and quick-fixers due to equipment misuse and negligence by others. For example, would a guestroom maid bump a trolley into the walls of her home? Would a cook close all the cabinets and drawers at home with his or her feet? Would the stewards throw all the china and glassware forcefully into their home's dishwasher? If employees were asked if they would behave in the same way towards equipment in their own homes, they would most likely reply, "No." Managers and supervisors must instill a sense of responsibility in their employees at the very early stages of their employment. Otherwise, mishandling of equipment will interrupt work processes and can cost the company, and its owners, a lot of money.

Career Tip: Hundreds and millions of dollars are wasted every year because of employees who take their work environment for granted because they are not properly supervised or accurately trained. All employees need to understand that the company's owners will have to pay for these unwarranted costs. That money has to come from somewhere, and most often, it comes from employees' bonus payouts.

149 Mini-Bars

Mini-bars in hotel guest rooms are one of the least thought out parts of the customer experience. They play a very minor role in the design of a hotel room and, many times, they are dysfunctional. Once designed and built, a mini-bar is usually handed over to the room service manager or food and beverage manager for stocking and set up. Throughout my career, I have seen many hotel rooms; however, only a very few are worth mentioning. While generating good sales from mini-bars is a completely different story, choosing the right supplies and properly setting up a mini-bar is another. One look at the number of coffee stains on the carpet sheds some light on this situation. Who is to blame for those carpet stains? Is it the guest who could not keep his or her balance juggling the coffee cup en route from the mini-bar to the bathroom? Or is it the food and beverage manager who decided on the awkward cup design that would make, even him, spill coffee over such a short distance. This is just some food for thought, and good luck to the poor housekeeper keeping those carpets clean.

Career Tip: Because a mini-bar is part of every room design and a carry-over "must have" from the past, managers will live with it. However, in 99 out of 100 cases, managers do not care about mini-bars because the revenue income from this feature is a fraction of what is generated by their other big operations. Your half a million dollar investment to buy these mini-bar units and load them will now sit idle for many more years, unless sales results are challenged or a passionate manager is found.

150 Children's Areas

Never put managers in charge of children play areas if they do not have children of their own. A childless manager will wrongly think that a few colorful throw pillows, some old and worn plastic play mats, an outdated cartoon DVD, and a bowl of cookies are sufficient. These young fellows, the 2-6's and the 7-12's, are sophisticated individuals. That is why they need a well thought out play area with up-to-date toys, a good play selection, and activities suitable to their age levels. Remember, if the children are happy, their parents will return to your establishment over and over, because the opinions and needs of these young ones hold sway over parental decision-making.

Career Tip: While this may be a trying topic for many, be assured that, if you attend to their needs, children not only have great influence over their parents (your current customers), but they will grow to dearly treasure your company's name. They are your customers of tomorrow and a big business opportunity awaits you; do things well now.

151 Trial Period Importance – Getting It Right

Trial periods, for the opening of a new restaurant or a bar, are very essential and effective ways to prepare front and back of the house teams for the real launch. Depending on the business's size, a three to five day trial period is recommended before opening to the public. For example, a 50-seat restaurant might have the following trial set up: Day 1, 10 guests for lunch and 20 guests for dinner; Day 2, 20 guests for lunch and 30 guests for dinner; and Day 3, 30 guests for lunch and 50, or more, guests for dinner. On the final night of the three-day trial run, it is crucial to stretch the capabilities of the business unit and, basically, crash the system. This will establish a good understanding of the limit levels for the operation and the staff. Day 4 is used to recap and re-train the areas, as needed. Day 5 is a day of preparation with no lunch service. That evening, you should invite 30 to 40 actual guests for a free trial. From there on out, good luck with your business.

Career Tip: Starting new ventures involves the efforts of many people. A new restaurant or bar will run more smoothly if you provide your employees with a trial run before your establishment officially opens for business. In this way, you will be able to identify areas that need improvement before you actually open for business. Doing so will be an investment in the future success of your operation.

---

152 Well-Oiled Harmony

A well-oiled team can be worth its weight in gold. Throughout my career, I have had the pleasure to be part of such teams, as well as to see others execute tasks to near perfection. It does not always have to be the big stuff, but a customer's smile is a customer satisfaction indicator.

Consider the medium-sized hotel lobby that hosted four pillars where four bellmen, dressed like British guards, were stationed. What actually happened was the cross-vision created by the presence of these four gentlemen. No matter from which direction a guest approached the lobby, it was impossible to arrive unnoticed without being acknowledged by hotel staff and greeted with warm smiles or to be offered assistance.

Consider, as well, a waiter in a restaurant, who was just about to pour the last of a bottle of wine into one of the glasses of a party of four. Two more glasses were also waiting to be refilled. Did he have to leave the table in order for his guests to obtain a fresh bottle of wine? No, he simply turned 180 degrees to where a colleague was already waiting with that new bottle. The entire action took two seconds and was a seamless service experience. That is blindfolded teamwork.

A LITTLE SALES AND MARKETING

153 David and Goliath

This principle applies to businesses that are small and independent, or sometimes not so small but still independent. The sales office in a smaller or independent operation might only be staffed with 10 personnel, as opposed to the giant chain that has 30 sales offices worldwide. While most small companies might use that as an excuse for not being as successful as their bigger competitors, a selected few will see this challenge as a business opportunity. As the David and Goliath story goes, the happy ending for many small independent businesses is to beat their competition: the big guy. This is possible with a lot of determination, a restless commitment to excellence, and hard work. With the right amount of determination and perseverance, the elusive goal of success is not so impossible after all.

Career Tip: Working in an independent business can be a wonderful experience for young and older employees alike. Independent businesses are versatile and provide a variety of playing fields and opportunities for their employees. These learning experiences are far greater in a small office than in a larger office, where bureaucracy and numerous layers of management make it sometimes difficult to execute quick decisions or materialize one's own ideas. Try to work in both establishments and you will see the difference.

154 Target Audiences

Depending on your business's nature, it is always a good thing to keep abreast of what is happening in locations near your business and within your city and region. It could be that a new office building, boasting many new tenants, is about to open around the corner, or that a regional travel agent office has suddenly received rave reviews and its owners are looking for a place to celebrate their success. The fact of the matter is that there are plenty of potential customers in the marketplace. If they know about your business, they will find you. If they do not know about your business, go out there and find them.

Career Tips: Target audience is a magic buzzword to many in the industry. However, too often this audience goes untapped or is incorrectly pursued. Having that special promotional idea is important, but knowing who to sell it to is even better. Every person travelling on an airplane heading in your direction is a potential customer and so is any person working or walking near your business. It is up to you to identify these audiences, place them into their correct market segments, and then go out and market to them. If you focus your marketing sights too narrowly, you might miss some golden marketing opportunities. Just because some people fly business or first class, it does not mean that none of the other 300 passengers are potential clients of yours, too.

155 Promotion Interaction

The success of any restaurant, bar, or room promotion greatly depends on the proactive interaction of the division heads of these relevant departments. So often, great promotions are established, only to fail, due to improper time management and shortsighted promotional lead times. While many organizations establish a yearly promotions calendar prior to year-end, the document is either barely followed up throughout the rest of the year or the lead times required to effectively promote the promotions are left unconsidered. Consequently, last minute promotion announcements will not bring the desired results. Operational people are very good at preparing and executing events but are not as good at properly planning them. Hence, they tend to be late and need numerous reminders. A strong and demanding PR person, with the support of the administrative and operational division heads, can make promotions much more effective and highly successful.

Career Tip: Oftentimes, people in different departments do not automatically speak to each other. Administrative and operational division heads must change that by leading by example with a solid commitment to ongoing interdepartmental communications. Relationship-building and team-building start at the top and trickle down to the rank and file staff. If all teams work well together and believe in planning, execution, and results, the effectiveness of promotional efforts can be vastly improved.

156 More than the Extra Mile

How do you impress someone who is a premier travel writer, journalist, and globetrotter and has spent the last 20 years doing nothing but staying in the world's best hotels and resorts for 300 of 365 days a year and who has seen it all? It is not easy, that is for sure. This is how the story goes: This premier travel writer, now a dear and respected friend, was already en route for a two-day stay at my luxury island resort somewhere between Europe and the American continent. Besides arranging the best accommodation and amenities, something else needed to be done to ensure a successful visit.

After a few sleepless nights and endless thinking, an idea was born. The idea was to tempt the travel writer to take an island tour on the owner's private yacht, visiting the beautiful islands nearby. After a light lunch meeting, the island tour offer was accepted and the travel writer was ushered onto the motor yacht. Little did the travel writer know that the captain had been instructed to take the long route around the east side of the islands while myself and a handful of people began a journey that was about to become an adventure.

First, we waited until the motor yacht had left the bay and was out of sight. Then, we immediately loaded antique furniture, ice carvings, floral decorations, champagne, and the company's finest caviar onto a second boat. We fired up the engines, held on to our cargo, and left, en route to a remote, uninhabited island in the middle of the ocean. Naturally, we took the western route to avoid being seen by the travel writer.

Timing was crucial since you can keep a travel writer for only so long on a boat cruising islands before it has visited them all. Thus, we rushed to our secret island destination and anchored a few yards offshore. Over our shoulders and chest deep in the water, we then carried by hand everything that we had gotten onto the beach. Once everything reached the beach, safe and dry, we started to set up our vision, which was drawn on a little piece of sketch paper.

When we were ready, we alerted the captain of the motor yacht and the travel writer's unknown journey began. Although hesitant to get off the boat, the first crew managed to convince the travel writer to walk ashore to check out the untouched island. Once ashore, the travel writer seemed confused to see a bunch of people screaming from a distance and waving their hands. As the first team with our guest walked closer and closer and their faces could be seen, we could see the emerging smiles and looks of revelation.

What was to be seen was a pure and untouched white sand beach, with an antique credenza gently set in the sand, filled with delicate ice carvings that each held individual tins of the finest caviar. Sterling silver ice buckets, bottles of fine champagne, crystal glasses, exquisite floral arrangements, a perfect blue sky, and a gentle ocean breeze completed this special impromptu set up. The next hour was full of laughter, great conversations, and a pat on the back for the team for a surprise well done.

157 Sales Promises

Sales managers make promises to their clients all the time based on their products and offerings. Thus, it is imperative for all operating departments to live up to the company's or sales manager's promise. Not following through on a promise — whether it be the fault of a junior or senior staff member — will erode the customer's trust in the sales manager and harm the customer's perception of the company. The result will be a sales manager who becomes cautious instead of confident about future promises, missing out on the business's full sales potentials.

Career Tip: Tangible or intangible, a promise is a promise. No matter how nice of a picture you paint for your customers, remember that once the sale is landed, your products better live up to your promises. It is great to show beautiful pictures of a property, guest rooms, or a restaurant; however, if those pictures are 10 years old and the product no longer matches it, you could inflict more harm than good. The same applies to photos of food that might have been created by five executive chefs years ago. Constantly update your picture library and do not sell what no longer exists.

158 Decision Power

Customers appreciate talking to a confident salesperson who has the authority to make decisions in the moment. So much business and revenue are lost every day due to sales people who are not equipped by their companies with the ability to commit to a course of action on the spot. If a company wishes to maximize its revenues and profits, it is highly recommended that it review its sales department rules and regulations in order to grant this decision-making power to its sales force. Sales people should be armed with clear guidelines regarding how much of a discount or how many value add-ons they can offer a customer on the spot before permitting them to make sales calls. This will make their jobs easier and enable them to close the business deal more effectively before the competitor's salesperson (who is waiting in line behind them) seals that deal. When a salesperson visits a company's major accounts, he or she should be accompanied by a senior salesperson, or even someone from the director level, to facilitate instant decision-making.

Career Tip: Giving your customer the anticipated answer, "Yes, we can," is a golden ingredient for any sales proposal. If your company does not enable its sales staff to do that, or if you are a salesperson who is not empowered to do that, your sales success ratio will be low, even if your efforts are high. In either case, review your company's current procedures or speak with your supervisor about this issue to establish a clear strategy with clear decision-making boundaries.

159 Backbone Insurance

If you still decide to do a cost discount promotion to foster more business, make certain your staff or team can handle the sudden influx of customers. Increasing a customer base from 20 to 200 can bring an influx of revenue and new customers into your business, but if your team is unprepared, your supplies insufficient, and your storage capabilities too small, you will quickly create 200 unhappy customers. The more prepared that you are, the better your chances of creating 200 new, satisfied customers.

Career Tip: The panic plan is never a recipe for success. All that happens with a poorly implemented promotion is that you give competitor companies an excuse to imitate your efforts. Your competition reasons, "They did it, we should do it," and in the end, both of you are the proud initiators of a shoddy, ill-conceived promotional event that brings the whole market down to a less than satisfactory level and overburdens the capabilities of your operation teams.

160 Those Viscous Promo Calendars

When planning promotional activity calendars, be sure to consider external influences and thoroughly attend to all the details. Before picking your promotional period, check the calendar for that upcoming year and make sure that none of your planned promotional days fall around holidays or any other dates that might weaken your efforts of getting the most out of your promotion. If possible, research your competition and avoid duplications or similar promotions during the same time. On the other hand, seasonal room promotions are offered by every hotel at the same time (sales and marketing people are usually predictable and disciplined with their routines), thus, your offer and value package must be highly competitive or extra special. Finding that unique loophole in a calendar year and launching a promotion at that time can significantly increase your chances for success.

Career Tip: Do not fall prey to developing a promotional calendar without proper research and planning. Plan well ahead and make necessary adjustments prior to launching your promotion. In addition, keep in mind that the ideas you had six to twelve months ago may no longer be relevant. Apply a consistent checks and balances approach to your promotional calendar and be open to revising it as needed.

161 Short-Lived Promotions

Promotions and special offers are important to customers and a good way to foster additional business. However, in most instances, they are short-lived and, at times, unsuccessful due to the lack of time and attention given to them by the personnel in charge of the promotion. Thus, managers should take a look at the sales statistics of each active promotion and consider either removing the unsuccessful ones or trying a new approach with the unsuccessful ones so that they might turn a profit. Gather your teams for brainstorming sessions and generate some fresh and new promotional ideas.

Career Tip: Checks and balances are important methods for avoiding short-lived promotions. Know what promotions have been done in the past and identify which ones worked and why. Do not simply repeat the unsuccessful promotions just because you have to fill a promotion quota. Instead, direct your team's energy into scanning the market for trends and assessing consumer behaviors, solicit fresh ideas from outside your department, and devise a successful promo calendar for the future.

162 The Manager of the Future

Current social networking websites, and other upcoming online venues that today's society wants to be connected with, are very important tools for your business. However, while the home webpage of many luxury hospitality companies includes a link to these social networking sites, typically no one on staff at the hospitality facility is designated to manage the company's website so the links and other information are not kept up-to-date. The new generation of hotels, restaurants, and bars should hire a social networking concierge to handle this important task. Some luxury hospitality companies already have social networking concierges on staff, but these are few and far between. As the world comes to rely more and more on social networking and other Internet sources, the need for a social networking concierge will grow and companies should make this a permanent department that will manage hotel, restaurant, and bar promotions, as well as customer relations. Hotel of tomorrow need dedicated staff to communicate constantly with this new generation of customers and keep them well informed.

Career Tip: To maximize your company's success, familiarize yourself with these new networking and communication tools if you do not currently feel up-to-speed on them. There are virtually limitless untapped business opportunities on the Web, but to take advantage of these new avenues of business growth, a company needs employees, such as a social networking concierge, who are well equipped and experienced in the dynamics of social networking and can focus managing this important business-generating tool.

---

163 In Search of 100%

A spa concept was once created, listing all the services and pampering experiences the facility offered its customers. This concept was then presented to an independent panel of people from different industries. While the concept aimed to provide its customers with a complete and satisfying experience, the feedback session that followed the presentation shed light on the weaknesses in the overall concept. The spa concept included everything a customer could wish for, from extended operational hours to an additional hour of free relaxation on the spa's ocean deck so customers could bask in the sun. However, the presenters had overlooked the fact that the spa was located in a very large resort area and transportation was required to reach it. This would make the spa more difficult for customers to visit and, possibly, more stressful for customers to find. Hence, the conceivers had only delivered 90% of their 100% promise.

Once the concept was rewritten, the customer would still be able to enjoy all the goodies and pampering the spa would offer, but the transportation concerns would no longer be an issue.

Now, the spa would offer consultations that would begin in the guest's villa, after which a spa consultant would escort the guest to and from their accommodations. This eliminated the customer's stress levels of rushing and trying to find the spa. It also provided the customers with the more personalized experience of being greeted at their own doorstep and escorted to and from the spa.

MONEY TALKS

164 Know Your Finances

Knowing your finances and figures is essential. If you have reached a level that allows you to participate in operational or financial reviews, make sure that you know every detail of your sales and operational figures. There is nothing more annoying to a senior executive than to question a participating manager about their departmental performance and not receive a correct, straight answer. In most situations, the senior executive is well aware of the department's performance and the questions are strictly geared to establish the executive's confidence level in the manager.

Career Tip: As soon as you reach a manager level, finance will automatically become a permanent part of your job duties. If you are currently a manager of a business unit that either makes money or is a cost center, your responsibility just got a lot bigger. For meetings and financial reviews, a formula for success is to be thoroughly prepared so you can preempt questions in advance. This will not only speed up the meeting, but it will also increase your supervisor's confidence in your skills and abilities.

165 Dollars and Cents

Some people might think that dollars and cents are nothing more than petty cash or small change. However, if you have ever broken your piggy bank, you know that small stuff can accumulate and become big stuff. This principle applies to businesses, as well. The small dollars-and-cents accounts should be periodically monitored and their performances evaluated. Companies employ hundreds and thousands of people, and if everyone saves a dollar, here or there, huge amounts can be saved by the end of the year, adding to that all-important financial bottom line. Ultimately, this cost-savings increases the chances for a greater bonus payout.

Career Tip: From the very start, occupy yourself with solutions for effective cost management. This challenge will only grow more complex as you grow in your career. There are plenty of areas in your business environment that run within comfortable margins and that do not affect the customer experience. Determine where the waste is and minimize it. There are many places where you can cut back on expenses to find an extra dollar, including tightening up the inventory in your storerooms and freezers and correcting wrongly or overpriced product selection. Doing so will strengthen your bottom line.

166 Cost-Saving Initiatives

To generate effective cost-saving initiatives, be sure that your company has a good chief engineer, an up-to-date executive chef, a knowledgeable housekeeper, and a clever finance director. These are the employees who either spend the most money in your business or have the most control over it. One way to cut back on expenses is to replace the elaborate fresh flower lobby arrangements with flowers that last longer. The guests will not necessarily notice the difference, but the longer lasting flowers, be they orchids or some other blossoms, will instantly save you 20-30% on your monthly flower expense. Another cost-saving idea is to replace the numerous tiny or high-energy consuming light bulbs that actually create heat and dust to LED bulbs. Doing so can save you up to 70-80% on your annual electricity costs and you will experience a fast return on your investment. There are many more cost-saving options that you can implement as well. Sit down with your team, research and discuss your options, and then draw up plans to implement them.

Career Tip: It takes foresight, knowledge, and intuitiveness to make the right decisions each year about what should be changed and upgraded and what can stay the same for another year. Stay up-to-date on rapidly moving technology, as these areas can save you a fortune. Although you may admire the large, beautiful chandeliers in your premises, you might never have seen the electricity bill the director of finance receives every month to pay for those shimmering lights.

167 Spreadsheet Tango

Financial statements, spreadsheets, formulas, calculations, and trend and market analyses are common tasks performed by middle and senior managers. It is important to take an interest in these areas early on in your career. For the novice, it is always a good idea to have a friend in the accounting department who is a financial expert that can teach you about such matters. Do not be afraid to seek help from such people in the early stages of your career.

Career Tip: Even in 2010, there are still many managers who still cannot perform the simplest of spreadsheet calculations and formulas. Senior managers will silently judge you due to the mediocre and low quality of the report that you just submitted. It is very important that you learn these tasks as rapidly as possible and find ways to produce a high quality report or spreadsheet.

168 Early Calculations

In the very early stages of your career, familiarize yourself with these important calculations: average room rates, occupancies, average checks in restaurants and bars, food and beverage costs, revenues per available room, multiple ratios, and payroll. These calculations are part of the everyday operations of your company and they will always be part of the information that you need to perform your job successfully. The more that you progress up the career ladder, the more important this information will become. Get a head start on learning everything you can about these matters. Doing so will improve your management skills and will help you to manage your business units more effectively.

Career Tip: In the luxury hospitality industry the calculations mentioned above are important to your career success. They will help you to make better, more informed decisions and they will alert you when something is about to change for the worse. Dealing with these numbers daily must become an integral part of your life.

169 Missed Conversions

Managers who close restaurants and bars and turn them into banquet venues are clearly incapable of finding the right concept for the place. These managers are very good at convincing themselves, and their superiors, that this is the best solution. It would be beneficial for someone to analyze the success of this endeavor by reviewing the occupancy rates, evaluating the revenue generated in the past, and estimating the new profits that might be generated by the new enterprise. Very often, you might discover that this change of business course might not have been such a good idea after all.

Career Tip: You must hustle for business success all the time. If your business in one area is so good that you must free up more space for it, then that is fine. However, if that business venture is not as successful as you want or need it to be, find a way to reconceptualize it in order to make it busy again and foster new jobs. There are many facilities that have remained untapped for years until, one day, someone comes along who actually knows what needs to be done and does it. Then, suddenly a fortune is made from a place that previously had been lying idle.

170 Speed Track Financial Knowledge

Make it a habit to understand, analyze, and properly react to reports. The more often that you do this, the faster you will be able to glean the information that you need by swiftly glancing over the reports. This is especially important to managers who need to make on-the-spot decisions in order to provide guidance and solutions to their subordinates. Business performance can be measured in many ways and, as the saying goes, figures do not lie. Try to spend most of your time in areas that are underperforming and help your team to turn these around. The more comfortable that you get with reading a report, the faster you will become at detecting areas that need your attention.

Career Tip: Reports are important for the successful execution of your job duties and they provide a wealth of information that will help you make the right decisions. When you ensure your commitment to the financial part of your job, success will follow.

171 That Common Happy Hour

Hospitality establishments offer Happy Hours either because competition is fierce or because a manager cannot determine what works best for the facility. If additional customers are generated and spill over into the non-discounted paying period, then offering a Happy Hour is acceptable. If existing customers only pay half-price for what they usually pay in full, then profits will suffer. A great manager or entrepreneur knows his market and generates ideas to foster that needed new business. Look at your demographics. Assess your potential customer base and the market trends and then devise a plan that works. If your idea does not work right away, change or adjust your concept until you find the right formula.

Career Tip: If a restaurant in New York turns over their full seating capacity four times in one evening and your business it is still struggling to fill a 5-8 PM Happy Hour slot, then it is time to go back to the drawing board and come up with some new concepts that will bring in more customers.

172 Receiving the Quality You Have Paid For

The hotel's receiving department plays an integral role in the maintenance of high quality standards. Every day, a dedicated receiver checks the produce and products coming through the loading bay and ensures that the company receives the goods they ordered and in the high quality for which they paid. If this is not the case, suppliers will very quickly figure out the gap in your organization and send you their B-grade products (this means a better profit margin for them). B-grade products result in mediocre outputs from your production teams and increased customer dissatisfaction.

Career Tip: The loading bay, or receiving area, is where all your company's goods arrive. These are the items that you ordered, in good faith, off your suppliers list but have not yet seen or touched. Trust is good, but checking is better.

173 Dropping That Price

Before you decide to draw more customers to your establishment by dropping the room rate or discounting the price your charge for brunch, do some calculations. Price dropping is not rocket science. Too often economic pressures crowd your fearful mind. Before you give in to your fears, prepare sliding scales and work out multiple scenarios with different price models. Then look at whether your desired numbers and, most importantly, your profits will still hold up if you implement your plan. If not, return to your desk and start all over until you have found the right strategy. Do not implement anything until you do.

Career Tip: Every manager has dropped prices only to discover, a little later, that nothing has changed and only profits have suffered. If you have made this mistake previously, do not do it again. Once you drop your prices, it is very difficult to raise them back to their original amounts again.

174 Upping the Ante

Upping the ante (such as increasing your prices) can be beneficial to your business's continued success. However, do not forget who got you there in the first place. Remember your suppliers, business associates, and second and third party relationships. Be sure that they can afford the price hikes you are implementing. If you forget about these "silent business partners," you have already broken a major rule regarding business relationships. One day, the sun may not shine as brightly on your business as it currently does, and if you have burned all your business relationship bridges, you might get very lonely, very quickly.

Career Tip: Forever foster, treasure, and respect your business relationships. Tend to both your new business relationships and your old ones. Yes, times have been good and you managed to increase your prices, which are now out of reach for those partners, but if you have stayed in good terms with them, chances are they will be there for you when you need them again. If you adopt the cold shoulder policy, you and your company's business will be quickly forgotten and vanish from their sales sheets.

175 Fundamental Failures

Fundamental gastronomic failures happen everywhere; no company, and no country, is spared. As the old saying goes, when times get tough, the tough get going. Unfortunately, there are not enough tough guys out there. Often these individuals are not tough by their own choice; it is more likely dictated by their company. Performance pressure that is caused by the reduction in the number of customers, large overheads, and faulty strategies can quickly bring a business to its knees. One not-so-sensible operator or owner will quickly adopt the price increase strategy to compensate for decreasing customer revenues while another slashes prices to such extend that, despite the reduction, only bottom-line profits fail.

Career Tip: Adopting clear and workable strategies can often save one's business or even make it more successful than it had been previously. Know your environment and your customer profiles, and then put your revised plan together and get going. If you overcharge for the same product for which they paid 20% less a few months ago, they will stay away. If you charge 20% less for the same product, they will question the quality of your product. Hence, you must always walk a fine line.

176 Room RES

An up-to-date room reservations department is one of your hotel's biggest assets. Thus, be sure that the room reservations management and staff are well treated so you can retain their services for as long as possible. These employees know the facility's room inventory and the layout of each room by heart. They are the people who can help the customer make the right decision. They are the ones yielding room rates on special occasions or during peak seasons.

Career Tip: Just because you cannot see the room reservations personnel, does not mean they are not there. This department is the nerve center of your business and employment stability in it is more important than you may think. If you have centralized reservation offices, find a reason to allow these employees to visit your properties or stay-over in order to become familiar with your product. Of course, if the person is handling tens or hundreds of hotels at the same time, this option might be more challenging. If this is the case, travelling to their office to provide the attention and recognition that they deserve might be a better solution.

177 Proper Money Channelling

Spending money properly is an important component of any business. Too often, money is spent in the wrong places and ends up in non-interest bearing inventories while the overall stature of your properties or establishments is degraded. For example, consider a food and beverage facility that thinks it must offer fancy specialty chocolate in its mini-bars. If approved, and depending on the property's room count, 20,000, 30,000, or sometimes as much as 50,000 dollars could be tied up in stocking these mini-bars and keeping the rest of the committed order in the storeroom. However, most customers do not opt for the expensive items in the mini-bar; hence, the money invested stands idle and the products quickly reach their expiration date. Instead, it would be smarter to use these funds to replace those fading flags at the entrance driveway, to replace those shabby uniforms worn by your frontline staff so they feel and look better, or to refresh that long overdue lobby or guest room upholstery. Spending money in the right places requires good common business sense, an eye for detail, and an employee and customer-oriented mindset.

Career Tip: Make it your priority to know everything that there is to know about your business unit and if money is available, make wise decisions about where to invest it so that it can be the most beneficial for making money for your business.

178 Forecasting Myths

There are no forecasting myths, only forecasting estimates. A good and reasonable forecast that is within ± 3% of your projections is acceptable. In the past, having a stable environment and economy made forecasting easier. Today, it takes a lot of skill, knowledge, and instinct to predict correctly which way the market will swing.

Career Tip: Work with historic patterns if you have too, but more importantly, stay abreast of what is happening around you. Speak frequently with clients, partners, and colleagues to learn how they are doing and how their business is performing during this period of ever-changing market dynamics. Stay up-to-date on regional and global changes and trends that can negatively affect you or have a positive impact upon your business.

179 Read, Read, Read

Try to read at least two newspapers every day, even more if possible. Select one newspaper that provides information about your immediate environment and another that covers the region. This will help you to stay updated on changing market conditions and trends that are close to you and it will also assist you in developing strategic plans for future business opportunities.

Career Tip: Nobody expects you to read every newspaper, line by line. However, take the time to carefully scan the headlines and focus in more detail on the stories that you feel are important to you and your business. I am not talking about the cartoon and sports sections — save those for after work.

180 Readying the Future - Financial Preparedness

If your business is doing fantastic and you are making great returns, prepare plans for the future. Plan for good and bad days, and even if your plan sits in the drawer for a little while, you will be ready when times change. Proactive mindsets are often the saviors of unpredictable economic situations.

Career Tip: A proactive mindset has saved many organizations from financial ruin. If your business is doing well, plan for new products or changes that will keep it prosperous. If times turn difficult, the speed with which you can implement the proper corrective measures is ultra-important.

181 Information Technology Myths

The IT or MIS budget of many companies is going through the roof. This is still one area in the hotel, restaurant, and bar industry that can be a little mysterious to the majority of employees (including high level executives). Most employees do not have enough working knowledge about high tech issues to sufficiently question an IT or MIS manager unless, of course, the IT department is directed by the head office. Even if this is the case, there are no guarantees. Make sure that you understand what your company's high tech systems can do and how they can positively enhance business. If your company's technological capabilities only provide detailed reporting, then a review of these reports is essential in determining their usefulness and identifying who will actually read and work with them. When properly used, technology is a wonderful tool.

Career Tip: Technology is critical to the success of any business; however, it often becomes outdated as fast as it is invented. To ensure that you know exactly what your business's technology needs are, obtain professional advice if necessary. The professional advice will hopefully assist you in spending IT funds more wisely in terms of the shelf life and effectiveness of software and hardware.

182 Be Prepared

Budget reviews, or any financial meetings, can be a lengthy process — especially if you are not properly prepared. To pare back the length of meetings, you must understand the needs of your audience. Memorize all pertinent figures and be able to formulate the answers to the questions that you anticipate that your audience may ask. Being fully prepared for a meeting saves you time, which can be better spent on generating more income for the company.

Career Tip: The more you know about your audience, the better prepared you will be for any meeting. Know the profile of the meeting participants and place yourself into their position. If the audience member has a marketing background, chances are that his or her interests will be in that region. If your board member served as the head of a banking institution, detailed finance and analysis might be the topics.

183 Quality Runs in a Circle

Always remember that quality runs in a circle. For example, take a moment and analyze a complaint that the fish smells or tastes bad. Imagine the cycle of a simple fish, beginning with the fisherman. He goes out to sea and catches the fish. The catch is poor and business is tough. Some of the fish do not look very good. Instead of releasing the fish back into the ocean, the fisherman decides to sell them at the market anyway. The merchant in the fish market buys the catch and includes it in his product offerings for that day. Although the merchant notices the poor condition of the fish, he decides to add it to the other fish when he fills a local restaurant's order. The restaurant buyer picks up the lot, brings it back to the restaurant. Then, despite noticing the one bad fish, he sends the batch to the kitchen.

The chefs receive the order and start to portion and prepare the fish for the evening's dinner service. One chef notices the unacceptable fish but decides to treat it with some seasoning and lemon juice to rid it of the smell. Finally, the fish is prepared and sent to the food pass for the waiter to pick up.

The waiter, familiar with the restaurant's dishes and quality standards, sees that this fish dish is not up to par and alerts the chef. The chef reprimands the waiter for challenging his skills and the fish is delivered to the customer. Finally, the customer complains about the meal and the fish is returned to the kitchen where it is thrown away.

The moral of the story is that all the people involved in this cycle could have prevented the bad fish from reaching the customer. In the end, the waiter could have been the final person to stop this cycle, avoiding the restaurant's loss in reputation and costly service recovery.

This quality cycle applies to every employee in every industry, from civil engineering to car manufacturing and from agriculture to conveyer belt productions. When proper attention is paid to upholding high standards of quality from the beginning of the quality cycle, a business's reputation is upheld and its customers remain satisfied.

EXECUTIVE PRINCIPLES

184 Designer Dreams

Designer dreams that become an operator's nightmare are very common in the hotel industry. Owners too often engage operators at the tail end of a project when most things have already been designed and constructed. While the finished product may look beautiful, the dysfunctional nature or fast deterioration of many areas places restraints on the operational teams and results in excessive maintenance costs throughout the lifespan of the property. Consider the architects that spent a fortune of the owner's money on elaborate roof designs and open arches only to realize, after completion, that this particular geographic region is prone to horizontal rain. This resulted in wet living and bedroom areas, as well as stained floors. Consider the case in which maximization of guest room numbers and public spaces ended in cramped back of the house areas, making it difficult for the staff to operate. This caused major safety hazards with hallways cluttered with equipment due to insufficient storage spaces.

Career Tip: Owners and corporations should make an effort to involve good, quality operational management teams in the early phases of planning. Of course, it is important to make sure that these operational teams are competent and knowledgeable. Choosing the right operational management team can save you millions of dollars down the road.

185 Details & Attention Matter

Every property needs a lot of attention and care, and if senior management does not take the lead by making periodic rounds and careful inspections, things may go unnoticed and deteriorate faster. Stained marble floors, peeled brass handles and poles, chipped concrete corners, and that hole in the carpet are all visual signs of a property that is not sufficiently cared for or of company funds that are being improperly channeled. If employees play their part in keeping the property pristine and well maintained, customers feel good, room rates can remain high, and sufficient profits will ensue, enabling a prolonged business lifespan.

Career Tip: You can only milk one cow for so long, and if you never feed it, its lifespan is limited. The same principle applies to properties. If you do not properly care for it and invest in its upkeep, its lifespan will be limited.

---

186 Spotless all the Way

Spotless properties are crucial to maintaining high quality standards, enhancing customer perceptions, and maintaining the overall status of a facility. It is not only spotless and well-pressed uniforms that make a good impression, but also the refined and well-maintained landscaping and gardens, the nicely polished furniture in the public areas, the shiny and functional chandelier bulbs, the glowing marble floors, and the stain-free white columns and walls. The hundreds of other areas and items in guest rooms, outlets, recreational areas, and the back of the house should also not be forgotten.

Career Tip: Every time I see a property with flaws, it hurts my heart. I am a hotelier who cares, even if the property is not mine but belongs to the competition. The quality of every property reflects upon the reputation of the entire hospitality industry.

---

187 Special Information

Information about guest histories is priceless. However, all too often, this information is left untouched and unanalyzed. The result is that a company may miss a special guest request and create an unhappy customer. It is very important to hire passionate professionals and create departments to collect this information so that everyone can be kept updated, well informed, and alerted to guest needs. If that special pillow, the perfectly prepared latte, or the extra towel is ready for the guest without him or her having to ask for it, your customer service ratings will jump sky-high and future customer returns will be guaranteed.

Career Tip: Guest details matter and, if recorded, these can be found in the company's customer history. How your employees use this information will decide the caliber of your operations and your business. Some companies have perfected this aspect of customer service while others, sadly, have no idea about what to do with guest history information.

---

188 Guest Comment Cards

Successful management of guest comment cards is time-consuming but well worth the effort. In most instances, guest comment cards are collected and then either sent to the corporate office for monthly analysis or assigned to divisional secretaries for monthly recording. The problem with this approach is that it slows down your company's ability to respond promptly to customers and it hampers your ability to keep your finger on the pulse of your operations and areas. If the general manager does not have the time to read every guest comment card, then the respective division heads should, at least, be required to do so. Another option is to have your PA identify the comments that need your attention and place them on your desk each morning. Some customers might still be in-house and their service concerns can be addressed before they leave. Others may have just left and may be positively surprised to see an e-mail response from your company before they reach their office the next day. Hundreds and thousands of guests stay in hospitality establishments every day and your commitment to response time is very crucial to the success of your hospitality business.

Career Tip: If you receive a negative comment and the guest is still in-house or on your premises, jump on the opportunity to respond. Do not let the guest leave without at least having made an effort to rectify the situation. The guest who shares his comments, in a good or a bad way, is a great customer who is trying to help you. Never disregard the importance of that. If you do, your business will be doomed.

189 Star Ratings

When it comes to ratings, stars can be given, earned, or sometimes self-proclaimed. Guests staying in your hotel will usually be responsible for your facility's international ratings. City guests who dine at and frequent your hotel are responsible for your local ratings. If you have received high international ratings and low city ratings, it is usually a clear sign of an impartial business focus. It is great to have 50,000 or 250,000 people staying with you every year but do not overlook the importance of the 300,000 local people who spend their money in your restaurants, bars, and banquet facilities.

Career Tip: Do not waste your advertising money to foster high rankings in magazines. The rankings of a company that engages in this practice are not legitimate and, most likely, their customers do not care about the ratings anyway. Instead, focus on the real deal.

190 The Local Star

You may have hosted many weddings at your hotel in the past year and noticed that the bride, groom, and immediate family members were happy, but it is also important to consider the experiences of all the other wedding attendees who might not have said anything to you. It is important to know whether they were waiting an hour for their next course or if they received slow service just because they happened to sit at table number fifty. The same principle applies to conference groups. The bottom line is that if you are considerate to all 200, 400, or 600 guests in your banquet hall and ensure that each of them is well tended, chances are that you will increase your domestic ratings. Reshape your service strategy a bit and the positive word-of-mouth that you create from all these satisfied customers will be enormous. Also, keep the full service circle/ experience in mind. Stationing the 20 smiling staff members at the entrance of an event to greet the guests is wonderful, but if this gesture is not repeated at the event's closing, you will fall short on providing a positive and satisfactory customer experience. Also, be sure to watch your departure protocol to avoid lengthy lines when people are trying to get their cars or make their way home.

Career Tip: Never take your local business for granted. Instead, make this a daily priority. In tough economic times, your overseas business will suffer and if you have not built and nurtured a local market, your rooms and restaurants will stay empty.

191 Mystery Shopper Reviews

Mystery Shopper reports are a common and unbiased tool used to measure a company's operational performance standards. These reports usually take two to three days to complete and the majority of companies conduct them once, or maybe twice, each year. Be sure to stay aware of what is going on in your organization the remaining 360 days of that year. If the cost of investment is too high to engage the services of a Mystery Shopper more frequently, find alternate solutions to test and benchmark your organizational and operational standards. The more feedback that you receive, the better prepared you will be to make the necessary corrections. Operations managers do not like Mystery

Shopper reports, as they could, potentially, expose them, but general managers, CEO's, and owners love them — and so should you.

Career Tip: Unbiased reviews are very important because they provide a more detailed analysis of your business. It helps the manager to pinpoint areas that do not live up the company's customer promise or deviate from the company's clear standards. The more often that you can review your operations, the better chance you stand to improve consistently.

---

192 Cyber-World Reviews

Website reviews can be as painful as they are helpful. In today's world, people use the Internet to speak out and while there may be some who use this medium for positive appraisals and encouragement, there are many others who use it to unleash their frustrations and anger. Social networking sites, and thousands of other sites, record the experiences of customer stays at, or visits to, your establishment. Most of the comments made in cyber-space are un-erasable and remain on the Internet for a lifetime. Cell phones have also become the ultimate tool for visually documenting everything from the happy experiences to negative encounters. The bottom line is that Internet reviews and cell phone videos and photos will be read and seen by others, consequently, influencing the decisions that they make about your business. No matter how much you solicit your staff to obtain positive comments on major travel websites, actual customer visits will play a bigger role in making or breaking your company's reputation. The best solution for good website reviews and comments is to deliver consistently what your company or property brochure promises.

Career Tip: Employees generally have cell phones and are well versed with the operational functions of these devices. Unfortunately, these young individuals very seldom think ahead and realize that how these devices are used by others can also affect the company for which they work. Cameras and recording devices are standard features on cell phones and can be useful in documenting a positive or a negative experience by customers of all ages.

---

193 Entrepreneur Concepts

Restaurant and bar concepts must fit the place and location. Hoteliers are often the worst concept people because they work in the food and beverage environment. They think they know it all, but many times people on the other side of the bar or the reservation desk know better. How many successful bar and restaurant concepts have mushroomed over the past two decades and are created by a group of young lawyers, students, or a collection of friends? These are successful because the concepts are based on their instincts and personal preferences. They design places that create an environment that is more for friends than for customers. Of course, there are the others who think they can copy concepts and expect it to work without a hitch. Unfortunately, this rarely happens.

Career Tip: Research the bars and restaurants that manage to stay open for more than three years. These concepts have a proven formula for success.

194 Concepts Must Last

For a qualified and experienced professional, creating restaurant concepts is quite simple. However, beware of over-the-top creativity associated with some of these concepts. While their fancy decor may be great to look at, they may offer creative culinary concepts and an attractive staff, and be highly popular when they first open, they, unfortunately, usually lack longevity. If your hotel has numerous food and beverage outlets, choose the themes for each of them wisely and be wary over the needs of the business.

Career Tip: When developing and writing concepts, keep the future close to your heart. Write down concepts that can withstand economic downturns and that can be sustained at least 10 years. Concepts must last and not fall prey to short longevity.

195 Opening at Once

It is a privilege to learn about, and experience, the opening of a business. In the hospitality industry, the term is known as an "opening at birth" and it is a wonderful thing. Opening at birth includes the launching of any hospitality business from full-scale hotels and resorts to restaurants and bars, which does not entail a soft opening. Everything is so well planned and everyone is so well prepared that the first business days are run smoothly, without buffers, and every possible glitch is easily dealt with.

Career Tip: Unless you decide to charge half-price from the day your business opens, it is fine to announce a soft opening status. If you charge full price, you must ensure that your guests receive 100% of what they are buying.

196 Trade and Sponsors

Being an official sponsor can be a very rewarding business proposition if the partner is chosen well. Being mentioned in a brochure, flyer, or mailer is nice, but it does not necessarily bring effective returns. If you are sponsoring something for charitable or community reasons, that is a different story. Any TV or large circulation-related sponsorship is generally a good idea. A free guest room, discounts on food and beverage, or other special offers can be provided at a minimal expense to your business and deliver maximum results. However, it should be noted that the longer the exposure, the greater the number of people who will see it. Being mentioned as an official sponsor in an e-mail blast might enable you to reach large numbers of target audience, but with so many blasts being received on a daily basis by e-mail users, the success ratio is usually low.

Career Tip: Before committing to a sponsorship, do your homework. A sponsorship must always benefit your business. If it does not, choose some other way to participate. Only be charitable when it is for a good cause.

197 The #2 Senior Spot

Once you finally reach the #2 senior executive level in your career, beware that you are no longer responsible for a single division. If, up until this point, you have specialized in one division and suddenly find yourself in charge of the entire hotel over the weekend or during the absence of your boss, keep this in mind: employees will now look at you as the person in charge. It will not matter to them if your background is in food and beverage, rooms, finance, or sales and marketing. It does not matter if you hold a fancy title. It only matter if your business habits are good enough to warrant your promotion. If your background is in the rooms division and the kitchen staff or other non-room related departments never get a chance to see you, you will not make much of an impression on, or be very helpful to, the operations and staff of the hotel. Do yourself a favor and become familiar with the people, teams, and areas that were outside the parameters of your job duties until now.

Career Tip: A career life is a never-ending journey of knowledge acquisition. If you make an early attempt to learn about the other areas in your business, teams in that area will be more willing to follow your lead. Doing so will help you make sounder decisions, without relying on your boss, which, in turn, will give your boss more confidence in your abilities.

198 Never Look Down

Now that you finally got that long deserved promotion, here the single most important advice you can receive: Do not forget from where you came! This applies to every promotion that comes your way in the span of your career. Far too many times, the individual who just got promoted experiences a sudden personality change. He or she holds his or her head higher than usual and he or she can no longer see the employees below them. The same people who were their peers yesterday and with whom they worked side-by-side unexpectedly become objects. This is not good management. Good management is when you use all your experiences, your wisdom, and your integrity to assist your staff to become better individuals and, hopefully, fill your position one day so that you can be promoted to the next level. It does not matter if you just made supervisor or senior manager; these rules apply for everyone.

Career Tip: The most rewarding feeling in a career is when co-workers from the past have only good memories of you. Even though there may have been hard times at work due to the demands of the workload, former employees will forever cherish a respectful relationship.

199 Island Assignments

It is highly recommended that a general manager or senior executive become involved in all aspects of a hotel or resort opening on remote islands. While your hands are already full with the conceptualization of facilities, service standard implementations, pre-sales and marketing campaigns, hiring of staff, and keeping on top of the pre-opening task list, do not overlook the facility's infrastructures. Ensure that you block off enough time to review these areas in detail, including storm drainages, sewage pump stations, irrigation, water tanks, landscaping, chillers, AHUs, emergency and evacuation plans, and other technical concerns and issues. Doing so will help you avoid unexpected incidents before openings and during early operational periods. Remember that technical breakdowns, hurricanes, or other natural disasters do not have schedules and, therefore, are unpredictable. For the safety of staff and guests, many incidents can be proactively avoided and disaster responses can be pre-planned.

Career Tip: Whenever you are assigned to a facility located outside of your comfort zone, take charge of the situation by getting to know everything that there is to know about the location and by anticipating everything that might happen. Do not take the chance of being unprepared.

---

200 That Viscous Hurricane Belt

Once I accepted a job on an island in one of the world's most beautiful ocean areas. While this region was prone to hurricanes, I was assured that nothing had happened in the past 90 years and that nothing would happen in the near future. I left it at that and started my job of preparing for a full-scale renovation and upcoming opening one year down the road.

While trust is good, checking is better so I began very early to familiarize myself with the National Oceanic and Atmospheric Administration's (NOAA) wonderfully easy online access and imagery and began tracking the satellite weather patterns. It became a habit that each morning, the first thing that I would do when I got to the office was to go online and check the NOAA's weather satellite imagery. On top of that, you are actually supposed to have weather alerts from the respective governments to which these islands belong.

Then the day came when a building weather front turned into a hurricane off the coast of Africa. Luckily, hurricanes move quite slowly, thus, you are able to track and prepare. This one gave me the chills for the simple reason that it did not follow the historic pattern of the hurricane belt. It stayed low and straight, coming straight at us.

I began to monitor the NOAA's site several times a day and, in the end, made the decision not to wait for a general government announcement but rather to take the risk to prepare in advance. Therefore, I instructed my teams and culinary divisions to bring food and provisions to a safe location on the property that could be used as a shelter in time of need. If worse came to worst and nothing happened, all we would have wasted was manpower and time. I prepared guest letters, information sheets, and task lists for my team in advance. We still had three days for the hurricane to change its mind and turn away from us.

Unfortunately, it did not so I made the call to alert guests of the upcoming threat, giving them sufficient time to board a plane and fly out of the danger zone. To my surprise, no one opted to leave, perhaps underestimating what was to come. Following the guidelines of a hurricane manual (each island hotel or resort should have one), I alerted and informed guests of the situation and possible timelines for actions. These actions included evacuation from their rooms and transfer to a safe location during the hurricane.

The hurricane's persistence in coming our way left me no choice but to finally evacuate all guests, staff, and anyone in need of shelter, which finally amounted to nearly 130 people. Once everyone was safe, my director of security and I stood at the resort's gate, looked at each other, and could not believe the extreme silence and emptiness that we were experiencing. What was hours ago full of life, motion, and noises had suddenly become tranquil and silent. In the distance, we could see the approaching weather front; it was time to join everyone else. I made a final call to my head office, alerting them of a possible but temporary phone silence. We then jumped in our buggy and made our way to the shelter.

Upon arrival, half of the guests and staff stood outside looking at the approaching weather front while the other half gathered in the shelter's restaurant, indulging in fine food and wine. Well, the shelter was actually a most beautiful stone building, solidly anchored in rock atop the island bluff. The winds began to pick up and the windows started to dent. These were clear signals for everyone, including the guests and staff of the restaurant, to move into the safety of the building's basement.

Once everyone was assembled and accounted for, we took a last glimpse at the resort's beach where, at that very moment, a large wave swallowed the newly built spa villas. The extremely well-behaved guests and exceptionally professional staff deserve kudos for their composure during the many hours that followed. Everyone was able to weather it and return to their accommodations only a few hours after the hurricane had passed. While the resort recorded substantial damage, everyone was safe and ready for a complimentary open bar afterwards. That, of course, is everyone with the exception of all staff who worked tirelessly to restore accommodations and clear beaches of debris, as well as a gigantic pool that was flushed to the rim with sand and seaweed.

A few days later, most of the guests returned to their destinations and one guest graciously wrote, "if ever faced with a similar situation, I would not hesitate to place my and the life of my family in the hands of this team." Always expect the unexpected and never leave things to chance when the safety of your staff and guests is at stake.

201 Owner Priorities

Profit-per-square foot is most likely more important to an owner than the typical RevPar or GOP. Owners invest in assets and they want to know what their returns will be on every inch they have built. Be sure to familiarize yourself with these figures and results, especially when the assets are not owned by the hotel company. This will also boost your aspirations to do better and be more creative in areas that do not perform that well. Ultimately, results will improve, owners will be happier, and you or your company will be recognized and/or retained.

Career Tip: If you do not have square foot measurements of statistics for your area, ask the engineering department for the information or calculate it yourself. If you are able to prepare trend charts and comparisons between areas, you may find many surprises and a completely new way of thinking about how to maximize revenues.

202 Every Owner Is a Good Owner - Relations

Every owner is a good owner. It is not up to the management company or the operator to judge who is wrong and who is right. Owners entrust their assets to both the management company and the facilities operator and believe in the promises that these companies make. Different owners have different sets of visions, but in most all cases, an owner's return and reputation are the key driving forces and formulas behind positive owner relationships.

Career Tip: The types of luxury hospitality facility owners who existed in the past are from a different era. The majority of today's owners are very familiar with other assets that are comparable to their own, and they have a set of expectations in mind before they build their facility. It is your responsibility to know and understand what these expectations are and to fulfill the owner's vision and goals.

203 Changing Owner Perceptions

Today, owners no longer build luxury hotels with multiple restaurants and bars. This is primarily due to the failures of their return on investment. It is unlikely that customer behaviors are to blame, as the restaurant next door is still full after all these years. Typically, the blame falls on unqualified management that was unable to run the operation in the way that is should have been run. Sometimes, when egos take over, the guiding principles of the business go out the door.

Career Tip: It takes skill and a good portion of customer know-how to create and manage successful hotel restaurant venues. Even by today's standards, that fancy star chef is no longer a guarantee for success, unless he or she is one of the very few that really stand behind their culinary commitment when signing their contract.

204 Twenty Four/Seven

After a long day of work, senior executives deserve some dedicated time with their family to rest and restore. Even so, a senior executive's job can demand their attention 24/7. While senior executives have spent all their life working hard, with many long hours and weekends preparing for this position, it is important that they periodically visit their business during their free time so that they can observe their employees when they least expect it. Hotels are a 24-hour, 7-days a week business and weekends are often some of the busiest periods for restaurants, banquets, spas, and recreational areas. A smart senior executive will make time to visit during these busiest of times. After midnight is also a good time for a senior executive to inspect the highly-paid overnight service contractors and say hello to the staff that is rarely working during the day hours.

Career Tip: As a senior executive, be aware that an establishment with visible management will automatically function better than an establishment without one. Frequent visits will also motivate your staff, gain you respect from your operational teams, and set an example for your subordinates to follow.

205 Status

While your fame has a lot to do with the hard work and time you invested in your professional career and the results you have achieved, remember to respect the companies that got you there in the first place. You are only as good as the name of the companies for which you have worked. If you ever decide to leave a place of great status, a part of your status will diminish as well.

Career Tip: Never forget from where you came. If you think that you are now another person just because you obtained a fancy job or are working at a prestigious property, you might be in for a surprise somewhere down the road. Stay progressive and always cherish each of the companies that nurtured you along your career path and that are responsible for your current success.

206 Top-Level Complacency

Now that you are in charge, ensure that you stay in charge. Do not get complacent about servicing the customers and accounts that are important to your company. Do not take a comfortable backseat position and observe from that dangerous distance. Your important clients and your staff still want to see you face-to-face and, most importantly, in action.

Career Tip: Too many times an important client, booked through the even more important travel agency that supports you, arrives at your door, only to be greeted and acknowledged by no one. It is imperative that you show your face, be free sometimes to host dinners (the more the better), personally greet them at the door of your establishment, and take the lead to deliver impeccable customer service.

---

207 Stubborn Perseverance

Stubborn perseverance can occur when you are charging a premium for your services and facilities, only to discover that the property or asset is in a tight spot, lacks business volume, and shows a fading bottom line. Staying your course and maintaining your existing strategy may work in good times, but in challenging times, managers often do not have the solution they need to stay afloat. At those times, strong leaders shine the most. Their many years of experience enable them to do the right things at the right time. At these times, exceptional senior executives show no fear; they have no problem rolling up their sleeves and getting down to work. While others hide behind the facts, wasting valuable time occupying their days writing explanations as to why the business is underperforming, a top-notch manager will take action to improve the situation.

Career Tip: Persevering to maintain "business as usual" is an attitude displayed by people who are not visionaries. The deeply passionate senior executive will look beyond the old strategies to find new ways to generate fresh business. If this involves doing the job themselves, then so be it. Their actions will positively impact the company's bottom line and strengthen staff motivation, encouraging them work harder and better to achieve the required results.

---

208 Ambitious Promises

Ambition is a great thing, but it can also be a very destructive force. If you are a junior, senior, or executive manager, use your great skills and virtues to establish accurate timelines. While your speed allows you to drive in the fast lane, be aware that your staff may not be as fast as you. Take a good look at your staff's strengths and weaknesses before you prepare a solid plan. Create a realistic timeline and then follow your determination to attain the ambitious promises with your team.

Career Tip: Before you jump to early conclusions and set unrealistic goals that are not achievable, evaluate and analyze each new job in detail. Too many times people have promised, "I will turn that around in six months," only to find themselves in the same spot twelve months later.

209 Leading all the Way

The term "leadership" is commonly used in the world of management. However, how many managers out there are actually walking that talk? Unfortunately, there are not very many. The arrogance of status quickly becomes a hindering block and before you know it, that nice guy is no longer approachable to the same employee he worked with for years. For masterful leadership, never forget from where you came. No matter how high your rank or title, spend time with employees at all levels.

Career Tip: Stay yourself, or at least try to stay yourself, no matter how much the pressure of a career lies upon your shoulders. In the end, you will only be as successful as your team and employees make you. Thus, value that relationship.

210 Following the Leader

If you happen to notice five pelicans flying in formation and following the one in front, you will also see that, no matter where and how often the lead pelican turns, the others stick with him. This same idea can be applied to humans and, specifically, to managers and employees in the luxury hospitality industry. Even in our world, if a leader is trusted by his or her peers and staff, this team will follow their manager's lead and climb mountains together.

Career Tip: The most beautiful thing a manager can wish for is a dedicated and loyal staff. These individuals are worth more than anything else. If you have reached that level of management leadership in which your staff follows your lead, treasure that feeling. If you have not attained that level of management skill, you might not be the right person for that team.

211 That Next Level Objective

One day, I started a new job as a senior director for a world-renowned top 10 luxury hotel. Although I was already hired by one of the senior executives, who I was slated to replace (code of conduct was at that time, "you can quit but not without finding your own replacement") I was scheduled to meet the busy and utterly social general manager on my first day of work.

I must have waited for a couple of hours, or more, until the personal assistant finally summoned me into the general manager's office. The general manager's desk was buried in big stacks of documents and it seemed there was very little time for a dialog; however, suddenly the focus shifted towards me and the general manager (most cherished lady in the world, besides my wife) looked at me and said I passed the good looking mark and asked if I had any questions. Although I had a million of questions, I was nervous searching for the perfect one so I simply asked a neutral question about my objectives.

The general manager raised her head, pulled down her reading glasses, looked me in the eye, and calmingly said, "The answer to your question is very simple. You are being placed in charge of an operation and property that operates at the very highest level in this world. Two years from now, when your contract is over; you'll give it back at this level, you will have failed. Anymore questions?"

I responded, "No, it is understood," crystal clear and then I left the office.

This general manager later became a famous CEO and also received the accolade of "Hotelier of the Year" from Hotels magazine. Still love and admire her till to-date.

As for me, this individual never again got involved in my work. She let me do what I do best: work with a results-driven, zero-defect, and error-free attitude. Our work relationship continued for the next eight years until we both decided to explore new ventures due to company infrastructure changes.

CPSIA information can be obtained
at www.ICGtesting.com
Printed in the USA
LVOW12s2131011116
511207LV00001B/377/P